a.k.a.
The Original Brown Boy

———

Paolo Javier

———

with art by
Alexander Tarampi & Ernest Concepcion

NIGHTBOAT BOOKS
NEW YORK

ISBN: 978-1-64362-072-5

Cover exterior art: "Malong" by Francis Estrada
Cover interior art (recto): *Untitled*, Alexander Tarampi & Paolo Javier
Interior art: Alexander Tarampi, Ernest Concepcion, and Paolo Javier

Design and typesetting by Rissa Hochberger
Typeset in Garamond LTC

Cataloging-in-publication data is available
from the Library of Congress

Nightboat Books
New York
www.nightboat.org

But paper and ink have conjuring abilities of their own.

LYNDA BARRY

CONTENTS

Aren't You A Mess   1

Goldfish Kisses   43

Restrained by Time   95

Last Gasp   123

Remain as Beast   183

Langa-Langa Boy   197

Afterword: Some Notes on bp Nichol
(Captain) Poetry, & Comics   245

Acknowledgments   263

Aren't You a Mess

These things I am going to say, not shout, for it is a long time since shouting has gone out of my life....

FRANTZ FANON

I was born on August 20, 1977

to parents whose names join easily

like the words

apple

tree

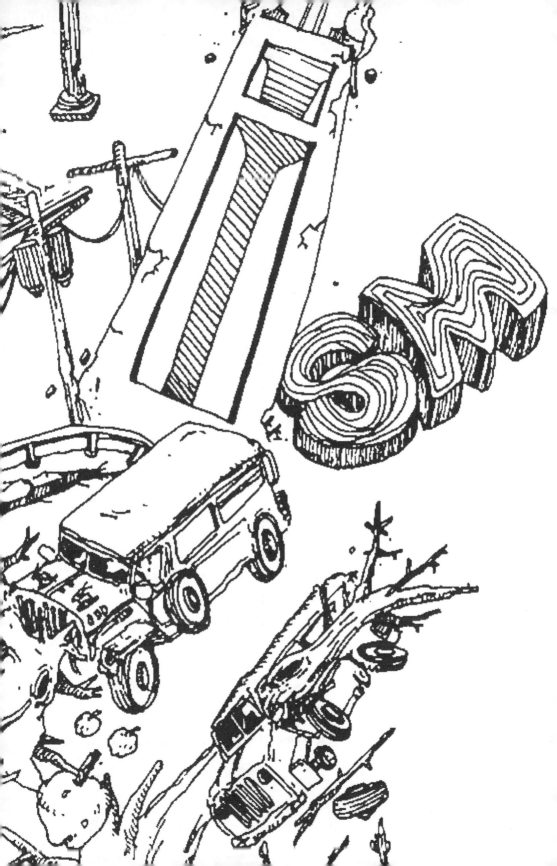

in Quezon City, where apple trees don't grow

& after a year (or was it three?)

of time spent paying rent for an apartment

in the city which was hardly the norm then

and likely won't ever be

they, we, packed

up a young family's belongings

& followed Rose's older sister's lead

buy a house

close to

the church

I

grew up in

Las Piñas

17 Galvez St; PhilAmLife Village

The first Pinoy you ever fall for
lives in PhilAmLife Village

in Q.C.

Maybe it was necessary.

back in the Philippines at an age you really could
comprehend

or distinguish that you had

come of age.

\- I want to be dominated.

the most beautiful boy

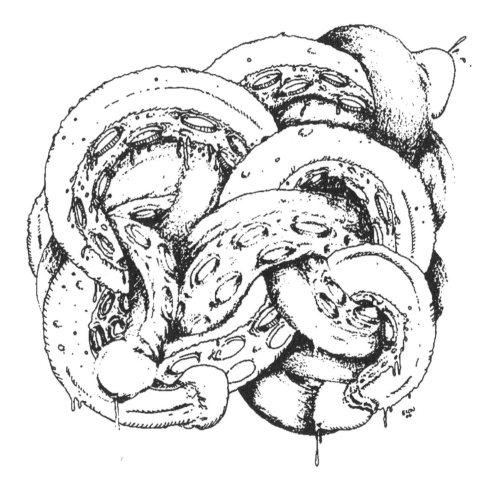

just like your typical Filipino man.

isn't

he

a

mess.

- You're nothing but a Tagalog teacher.

I remember

the   terrible moment

leaving

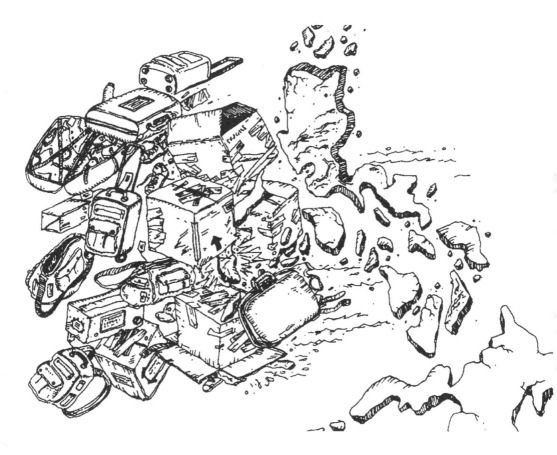

Manila is only outwardly you.

Monkey Boy! Monkey! Monkey!

I worried

I was happy

I'm not so worried

I think

born

in

America

Fil Am

falling

in love

with

typical

Filipino

all

over

.

again.

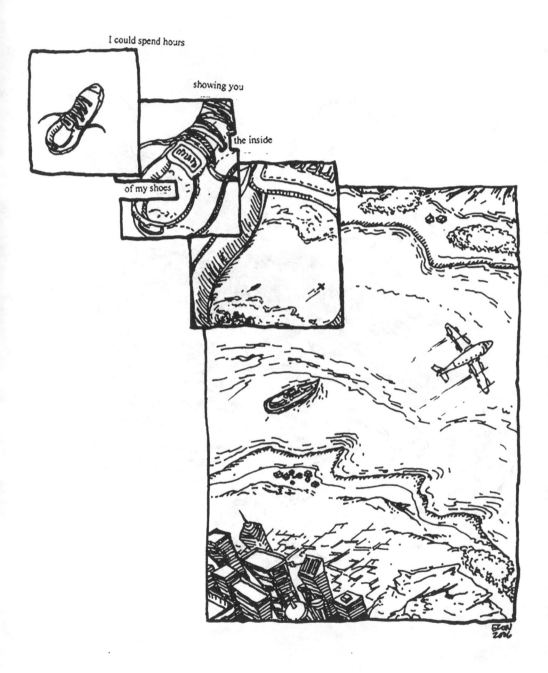

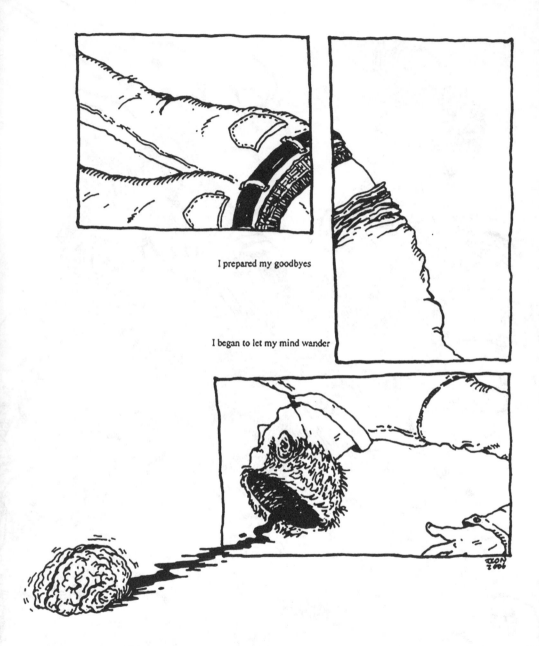

I prepared my goodbyes

I began to let my mind wander

Goldfish
Kisses

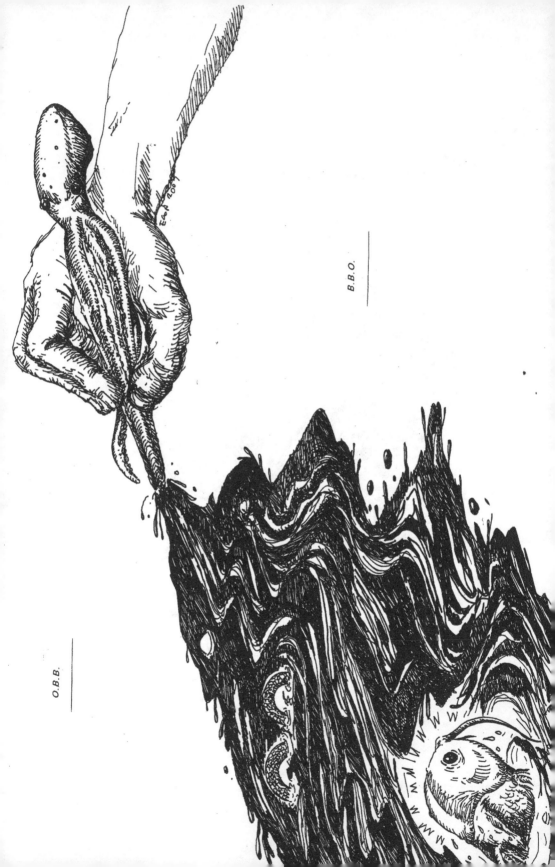

O.B.B.

B.B.O.

LIFE

TWILO

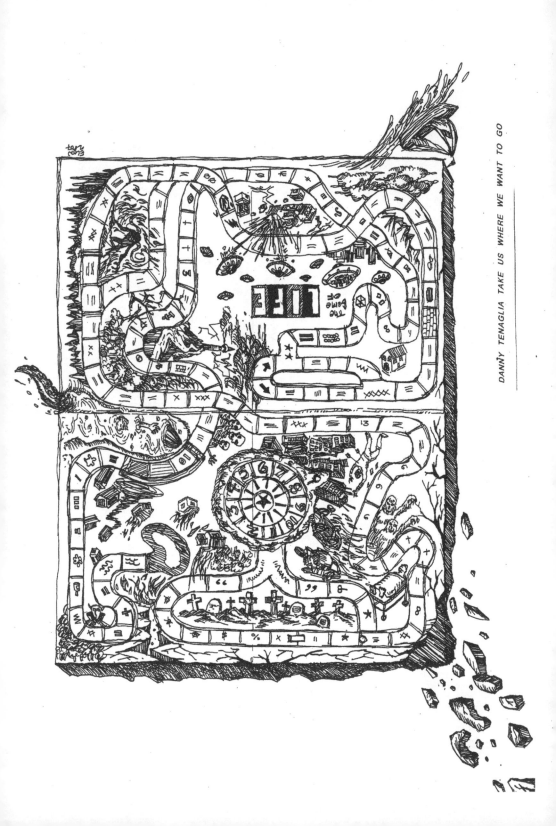

HORRIBLE FACE RECOGNITION

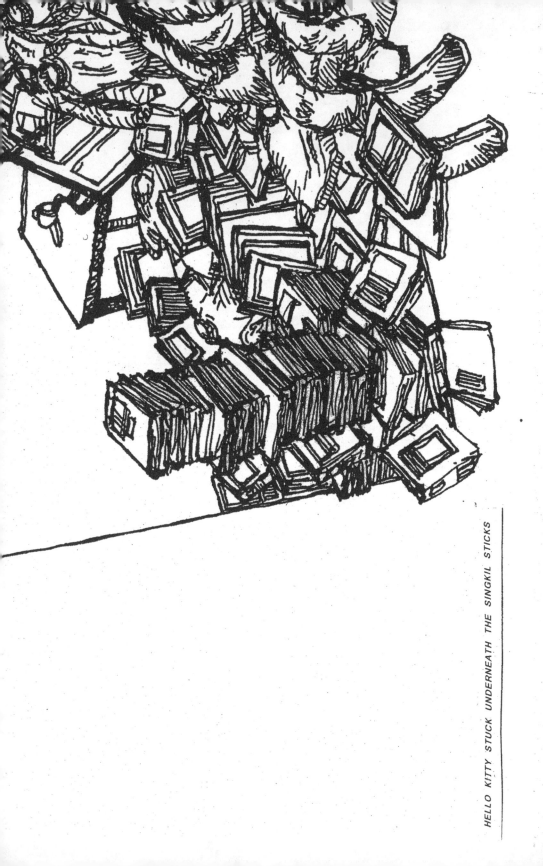

HELLO KITTY STUCK UNDERNEATH THE SINGKIL STICKS

COOK WITH KATIE

CALL YOUR VOICE MAIL

LEAVE NOTES

LEAVE YOUR RED PENS ALL OVER THE APARTMENT

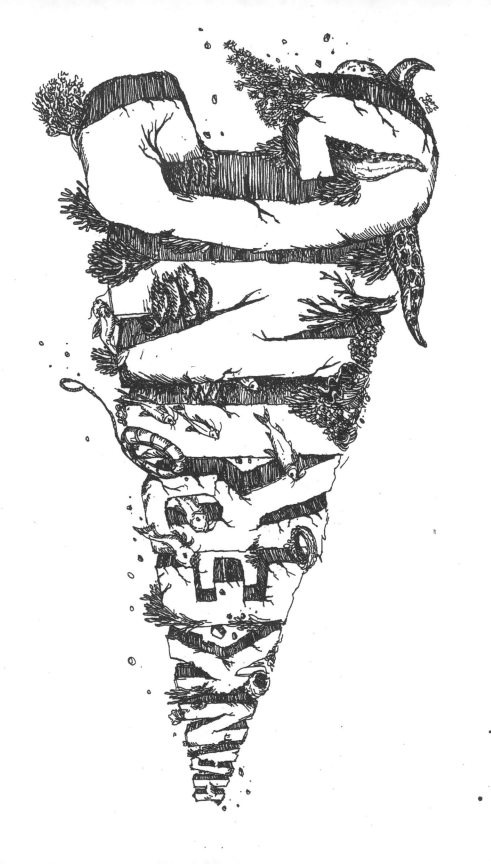

SPOIL LULU IN THE LOFT

TALK LIKE HICKS IN THE LOFT

BJORK

PSYCHEDELIC FURS

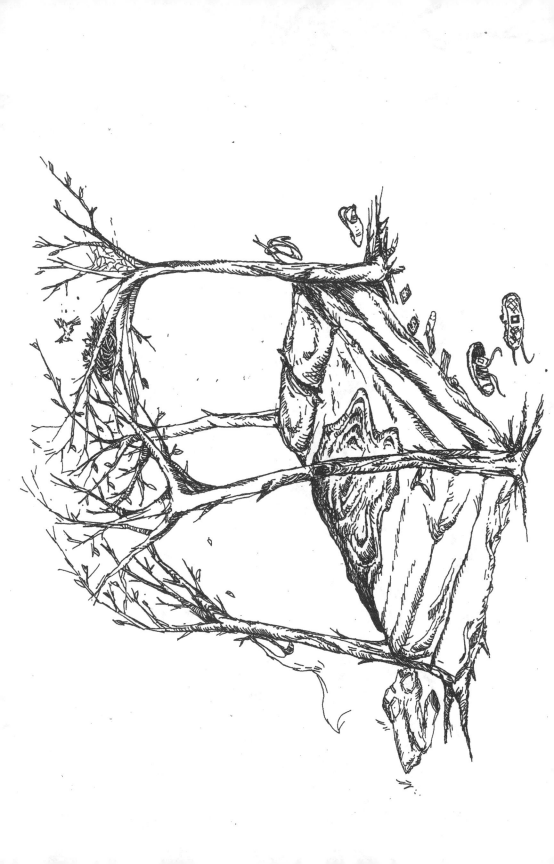

HORRIBLE FACE RECOGNITION

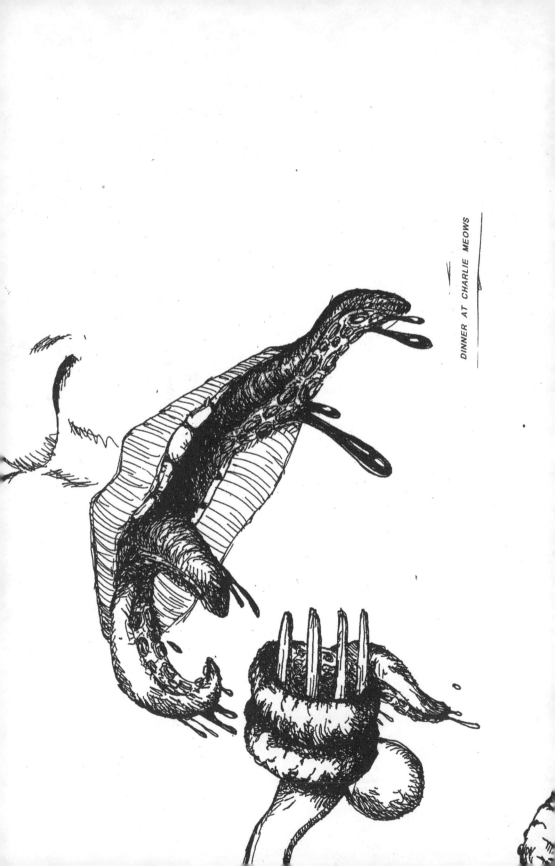

DINNER AT CHARLIE MEOWS

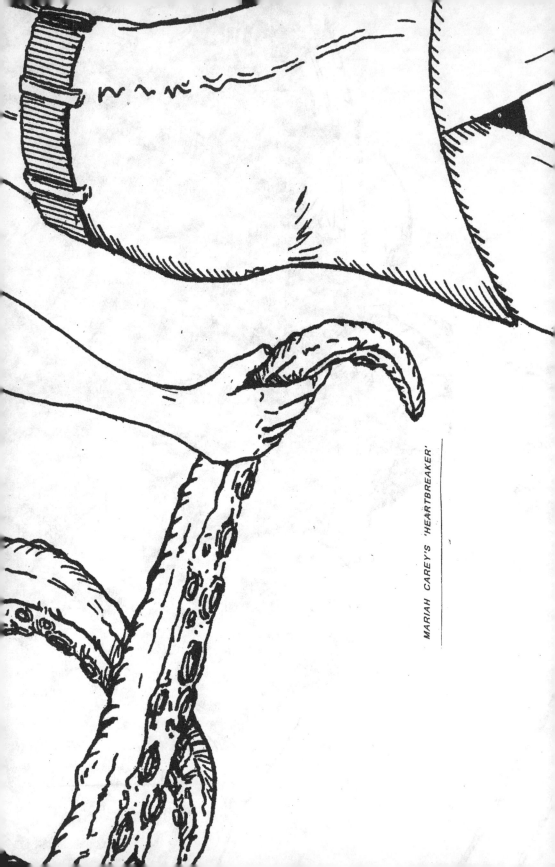

MARIAH CAREY'S 'HEARTBREAKER'

DANCE IN MY ROOM
_____

FIND SONGS ON NAPSTER
_____

'32 FLAVORS AND THEN SOME'

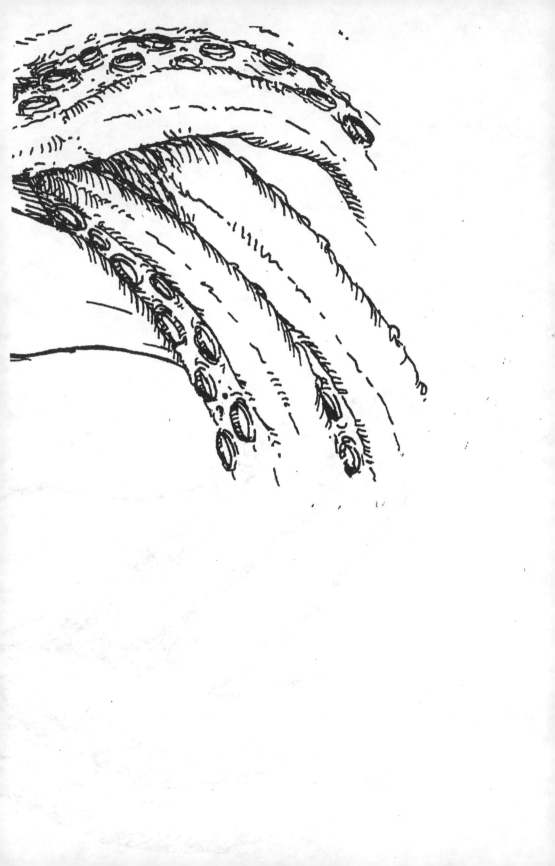

HOT FUDGE SUNDAES
_____

CHOCOLATE ECLAIRS
_____

"CHOCOLATE MUKHA"

"BIG ISDA"

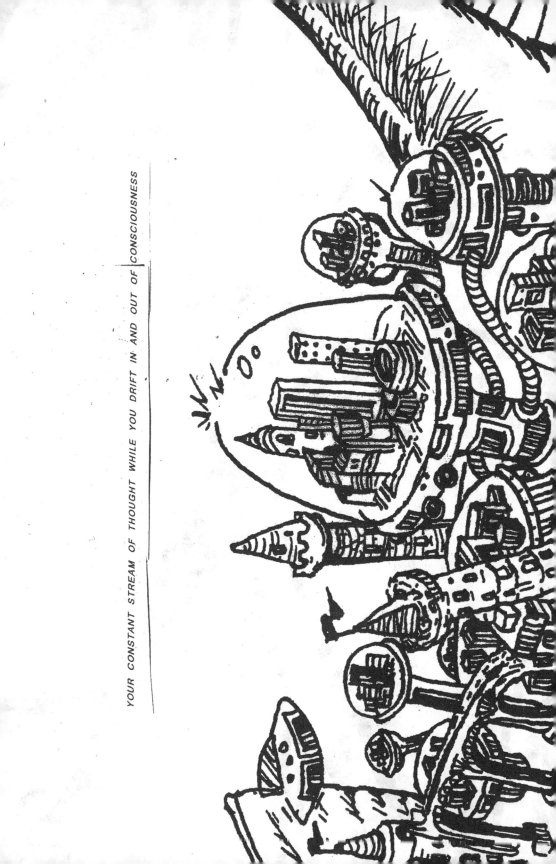

YOUR CONSTANT STREAM OF THOUGHT WHILE YOU DRIFT IN AND OUT OF CONSCIOUSNESS

SHARE COFFÈE

"PRETTY LADY"

VISIT MY HOUSE FOR THE FIRST TIME

MY LOLA AND MY TOWN

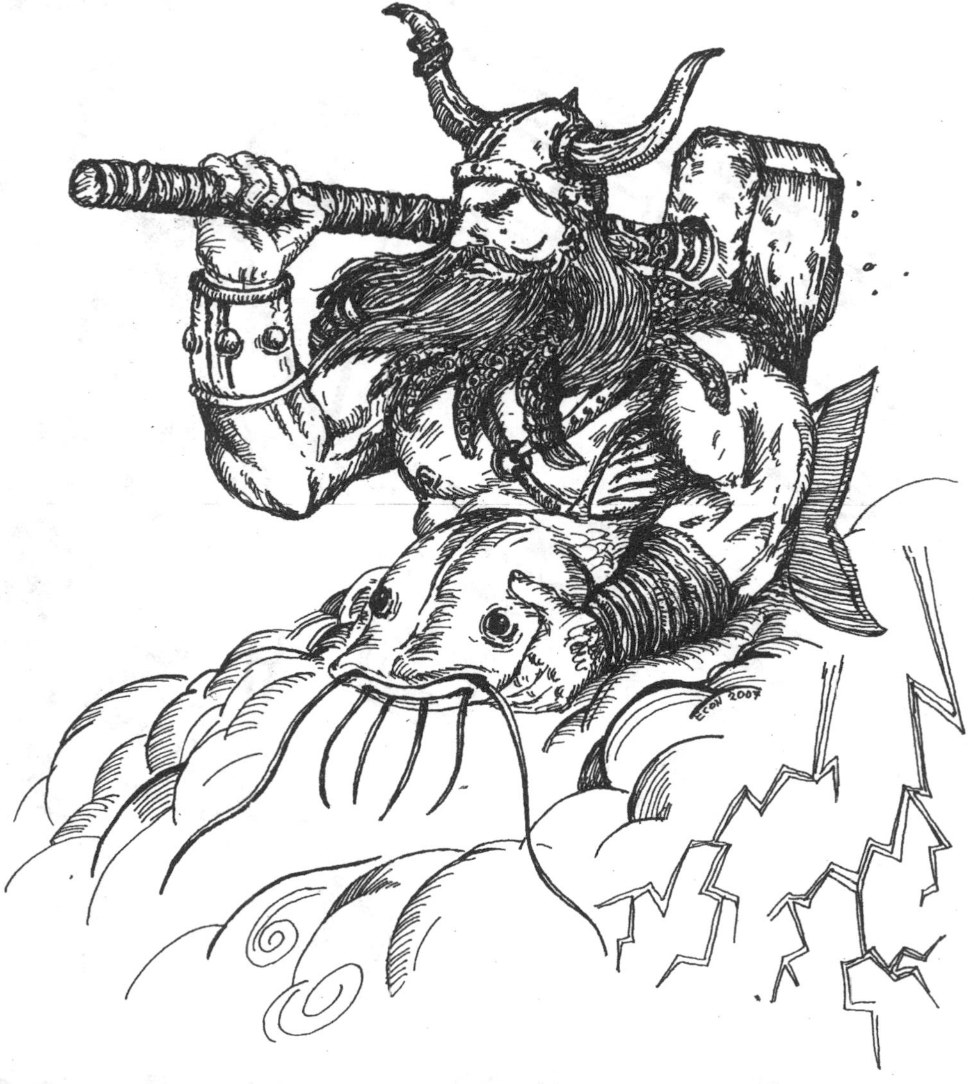

SPEND TIME WITH THOR

DROP ME OFF ON FIRST DAY AT WORK

MEET FOR LUNCH

AVENUE A SUSHI

LE BATEAU IVRE

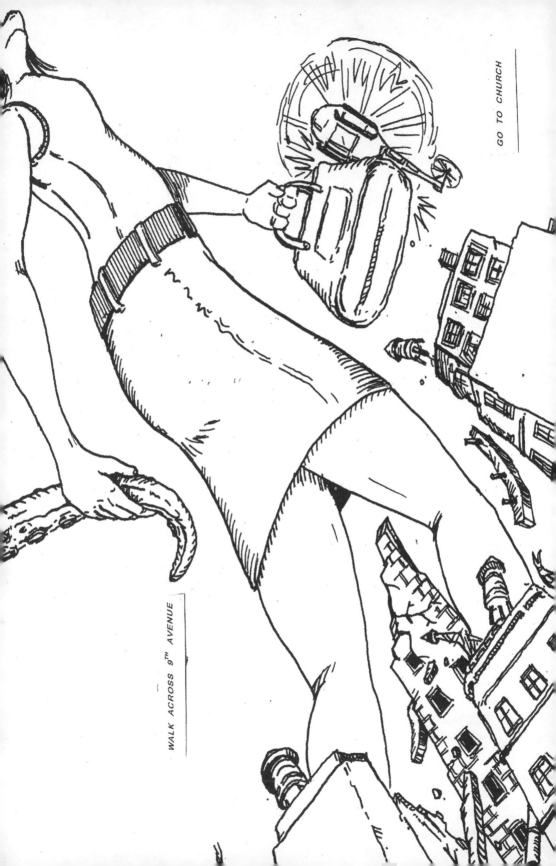

STARE IN AWE OF 101 ST MARKS PLACE

"I GO ON LOVING YOU LIKE WATER"

QUOTE YOUR POEMS WHEN WE FIGHT

MY LAUGH IS BEGINNING TO SOUND LIKE YOURS

MY STALKERS TED BERRIGAN,

FRANK O'HARA,

ROBERT CREELEY

PAOLO JAVIER

AND

ERNEST CONCEPCION

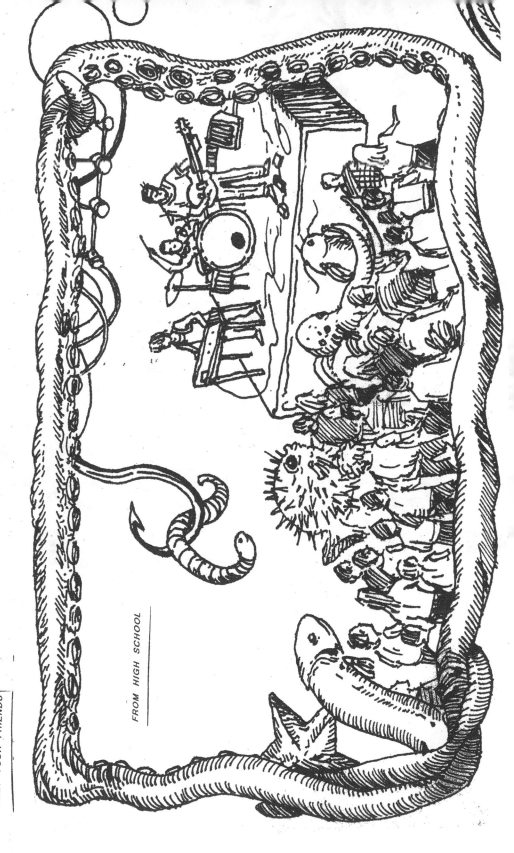

MEET YOUR FRIENDS

FROM HIGH SCHOOL

WONDER

WATCH YOU

GET A

HAIRCUT

FROM NINO

WINDOWSHOP

THUMB WRESTLING

OH THESE PEARL EARRINGS

YOUR FUNKY SHIRT _____

YOUR SCENT _____

YOUR LAUGH

YOUR PATIENCE

YOUR KINDNESS

YOUR ART OPENING

MY POEMS BUT NOT REALLY POEMS

OUR CATFISH CRAVING.

OUR GOLDFISH KISSES.

Restrained by Time

"Not me. Not that."

JULIA KRISTEVA

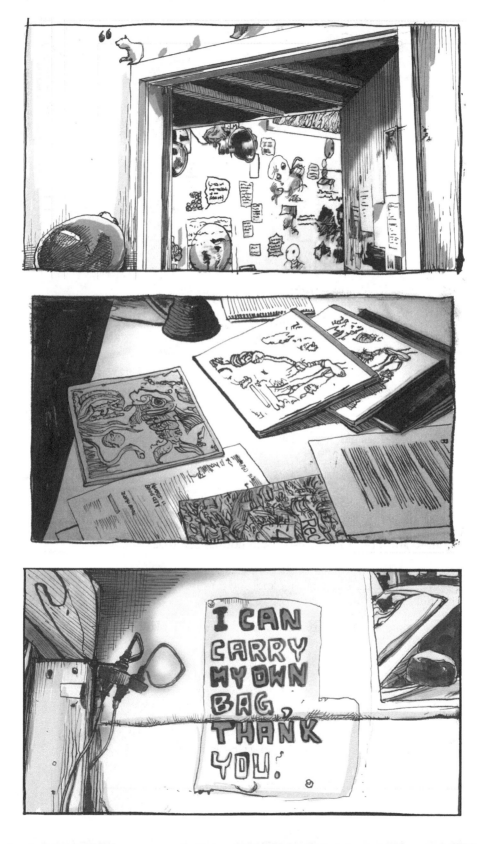

SHARPER THAN A SERPENT'S TOOTH

———

I

A Yankee Soldier and MB, aka Monkey Boy, come upon a well. One grand wave of patriotism answering Uncle Sam—your narrator's—call to arms. But the explosion will not happen today.

"You look like a mongoloid!" says Yankee Soldier.

Both want to have the plant, to divide the plant into two, and then assign.

"My final prayer: O my body, make of me always someone who questions!" says MB.

And to think it was *I* who gave them the gun!

"I'll call you Big Forehead Boy, ok?" says Yankee Soldier. "Let's be halves for the both of us."

The Sphinx has spoken! At the conclusion of this study, I want the world to recognize, with me, the open door of every consciousness. Nakakaraos rin.

Yankee Soldier desires the top part, a part which is golden. He sneers: "Guess I'll keep it!"

(I do not come with timeless truths. Your move, General Otis!)

"MB! BFB! Turn around!" says Yankee Soldier.

"Was my freedom not given to me then in order to build the world of the You?" MB says. "And since I thought of it, I get to choose which half."

Yankee Soldier sets to work cutting the banana plant. "Gosh! I wish they wouldn't come quite so many in a bunch." He leaves the ugly stump to Monkey Boy. "But if I've got to take them, I guess I can do as well by them as I've done by the others!"

It would seem that this fact has not been given sufficient attention by those who have discussed the question.

"Aren't we good friends?" MB asks. "My consciousness is not illuminated with ultimate radiances. Will you let--"

Can the missionary teach this old savage? Call me when you get there!

"I've gotten what I want out of you," says Yankee Soldier.

MB does not complain. "Allow me to thank you for the very cordial support and encouragement you have given me," he says.

There is of course the moment of "being for others," of which Hegel speaks, but every ontology is made unattainable in a colonized and civilized society. Are you going to lock up or will I do it myself?

"Our halves of the plant," says Yankee Soldier. "I get to keep whatever of yours."

The first step towards lightening the White Man's Burden is through teaching the virtues of cleanliness. Nevertheless, in complete composure, I think it would be good if certain things were said.

"Goodbye, then," MB says.

"No!" snaps Yankee Soldier. "We'd agreed to stick to what comes of my half and you get to keep whatever comes."

Still scolding. Letting his light shine. Recommended by hoar frost. Horrible nightmare of a worthy gentleman. As long as Monkey Boy is among his own, he will have no occasion, except in minor internal conflicts, to experience his being through others.

"Why do you have to be so dramatic?" says Yankee Soldier. "Is it because of the radio or of me? You have your moods too you know."

II

After finishing off all the bananas, Monkey Boy plants some
more fruit. Everybody is against imperialism. Now, here's Me and
the Yankee Soldier and the Filipino. What more do *youse* want?

"For it is a long time since shouting has gone out of my life,"
MB says. "I wanted to be the one to come up with it. The top part
of the plant with the hope of growing with his half of the plant at all
as it was still the banana plant could not grow roots, and thus it grew
to be another beautiful banana having twice as many bananas as he
had been able near his full-grown banana plant."

We'd agreed Monkey Boy went home and plotted. Is a potent fac-
tor in brightening the dark corners of the earth as civilization advances,
while amongst the cultured of all nations it holds the highest
place--toilet soap?

"Now the fragments are being put together by another self," MB says.

"Are we gonna get married soon?" says Yankee Soldier.

"I...burst apart," MB says.

"Say, young fellow!" says Yankee Soldier. "You've behaved pretty well; but some of your antics are suspicious. Just remember that I've got my eye on you!"

A good natured hint! The Yankee Soldier did not have to do any rooting to the ground as a stump. But the top part shriveled up and died. The Yankee's stump, on the plant, and soon enough it makes Monkey Boy drool to extract from what had been his half.

"Get out, you old stiff," MB says. "I won this war myself."

How sharper than a serpent's tooth to have a thankless child!

"So very long..."

"Who's to say we'll be together then?" says Yankee Soldier.

"I am indignant. I demand an explanation. Nothing is happening."

My new caught anthropoid, holding his end up tonight and stealing the bananas straight from the breach of friendship. Yankee Soldier waits until Monkey Boy sets low to the ground, laying sharp pebbles. Monkey Boy jumps down from the plant after having so many places all at once! In fact, it is within a coconut's throw! You've got to jump through, and the sooner you do it the better!

"But just as I reached the other side, I stumbled, and the movements, the attitudes, the glances of the other fixed me there, in the sense in which a chemical solution is fixed by a dye," MB says.

"Shut up!" says Yankee Soldier. "When I get married, I'm going to live in a big house, so I can get away from my spouse for a while."

"Why write this book?" MB says. "Noone has asked for it."

It's really most extraordinary what training will do. Why, only the other day I thought this monkey unable to support itself. Yankee Soldier would not let MB come anywhere to stick to our halves of the plant. The flag that Dewey hosts on Manila shall never come down.

"Your attention is a liberation, running over my body suddenly abraded into nonbeing, endowing me once more with an agility that I had thought lost, and by taking me out of the world, restoring me to it," MB says.

(Ladies and gentlemen--enter Yankee Nurse!)

"Well, what should I do now?" she asks.

For starters, give MB another dose of shrapnel with a moderate charge of cavalry, then a daily injection of rapid fire. I am thinking of grinding your ashes. I am also thinking of throwing you into a touch of saltwater!

"There's plenty of room at the table, why not ask the hungry little fellow to sit down?" says Yankee Nurse.

"Especially those to whom it is directed," MB says. "I don't want to love anymore. Relationships end anyway. Sealed into this crushing objecthood, I turn beseechingly to others."

"U.S. Citizen?" says Yankee Nurse.

"Not much," MB says.

"Guess I'll have to make a subject of him," mutters Yankee Nurse.

Monkey Boy decides to sneak into Yankee Soldier's yard plant. But Yankee Soldier has been prepared for such a climb. Too high up to be aware of anything gone all around the roots of the plant, Monkey Boy eats as many bananas as he can, and us stung.

"Well?" says Yankee Soldier, taking up the first installment of the white man's burden.

"Well I reply quite calmly that there are too many idiots in this world," MB says. "And having said it, I have the burden of proving it."

"I can't even be around you for too long," says Yankee Soldier.

"I came into the world imbued with the will to find a meaning in things, my spirit filled with the desire to attain to the source of the world," MB says.

A slight addition to the white man's burden! Down to the seashore and flung the screaming. The trouble is you petted him. What he needs is the rod. Kill everyone over ten.

"You mean 'DIRTY NEGRITO?'" MB says.

"I need you," says Yankee Soldier. "I realized on the way here that you're my raison d'etre. I don't know what it's like to be on my own anymore."

MB clears his throat. "Toward a new humanism...?"

"William, I can never digest this mess without straining my constitution," says Yankee Soldier. "Now I can do what I please with 'em."

MB is furious! Yankee Soldier hunted all around for thee, grabbed the slow-paced creature by its shell so t'would be killed.

"Be good, or you will be dead!" says Yankee Nurse. "Speaking from experience."

"From this other form, from this original complex in its pure state that supposedly characterized this Monkey Boy's mentality throughout the whole precolonial period, it appears to me that you lack the slightest basis on which to ground any conclusion applicable to the situation, the problems, or the potentialities of this Monkey Boy in the present time."

"I think that's part of the reason why I wanted to move to Hawai'I," says Yankee Soldier. "To be by myself for once."

Understanding among men!

"But as we had been good friends, I will let you choose your difficult shell in a mortar," MB says. "In which manner would you like to die?"

I'm not sure that I got a bargain when I paid twenty million dollars! If one adds that many Europeans go to the colonies because it is possible for them to grow rich quickly there, that with rare exceptions the colonial is a merchant, or rather a trafficker, one will have grasped the psychology of the man who arouses in the autochthonous population "the feeling of inferiority".

"I think I'm going to die soon," says Yankee Nurse. "Let's eat lots of vegetables today."

"Mankind, I believe in you," MB says. "Race prejudice, to understand and to love..From all sides dozens and hundreds of pages assail..."

"The flag must stay put," says Yankee Soldier. "American Filipinos and Native Filipinos will have to submit."

"Grind me to ashes. For I cannot...aha! So you hate saltwater!"

MB races off. How can I teach *this* self government? The critter barks and wags at the same time. Which end of him is lyin? I reckon I'll have to squeeze a little harder to hold em down.

"You invest the hero, who is white, with all his own aggression-- at that age closely linked to sacrificial dedication, a sacrificial dedication permeated with sadism. An eight-year-old child who offers a gift, even to an adult, cannot endure."

"I think the problem was that I liked you more than you liked me," says Yankee Nurse. "I just felt like kissing you like that. How come you don't kiss me anymore? MB--could you lie down next to me?

I am sorry that Yankee Nurse has told us nothing about her dreams. Darn the crittur! MB doesn't seem to like this imperial business. A flailing tortoise in the water, as far away as this monkey says, thinking that he had dealt the tortoise.

"Make me an offer, gentlemen!" says Yankee Nurse." It is always a question of compromising with the desire for a world without men.

"I think I do," MB says.

"MB--could you lie down next to me?!"

That would have made it easier to reach her unconscious. Give it to him, Yankee Nurse! Spare the rod and spoil the child, you know! Strong arms could manage. Shake, and you will boss the whole world.

"There is identification," says Yankee Soldier. "Adopt a white man's attitude. That's why you call it your first love. So you can make all the mistakes you want."

I am sorry that MB has told us nothing about his dreams. That would have made it easier to reach his unconscious. Spare the rod and spoil the child, you know! The ultimate revenge for spiting his cleverness.

Then try to imagine the barbarous Filipino enjoying the advantage of American civilization. Identifies himself with the explorer, the bringer of civilization, the white man who carries truth to savages--an all-white truth.

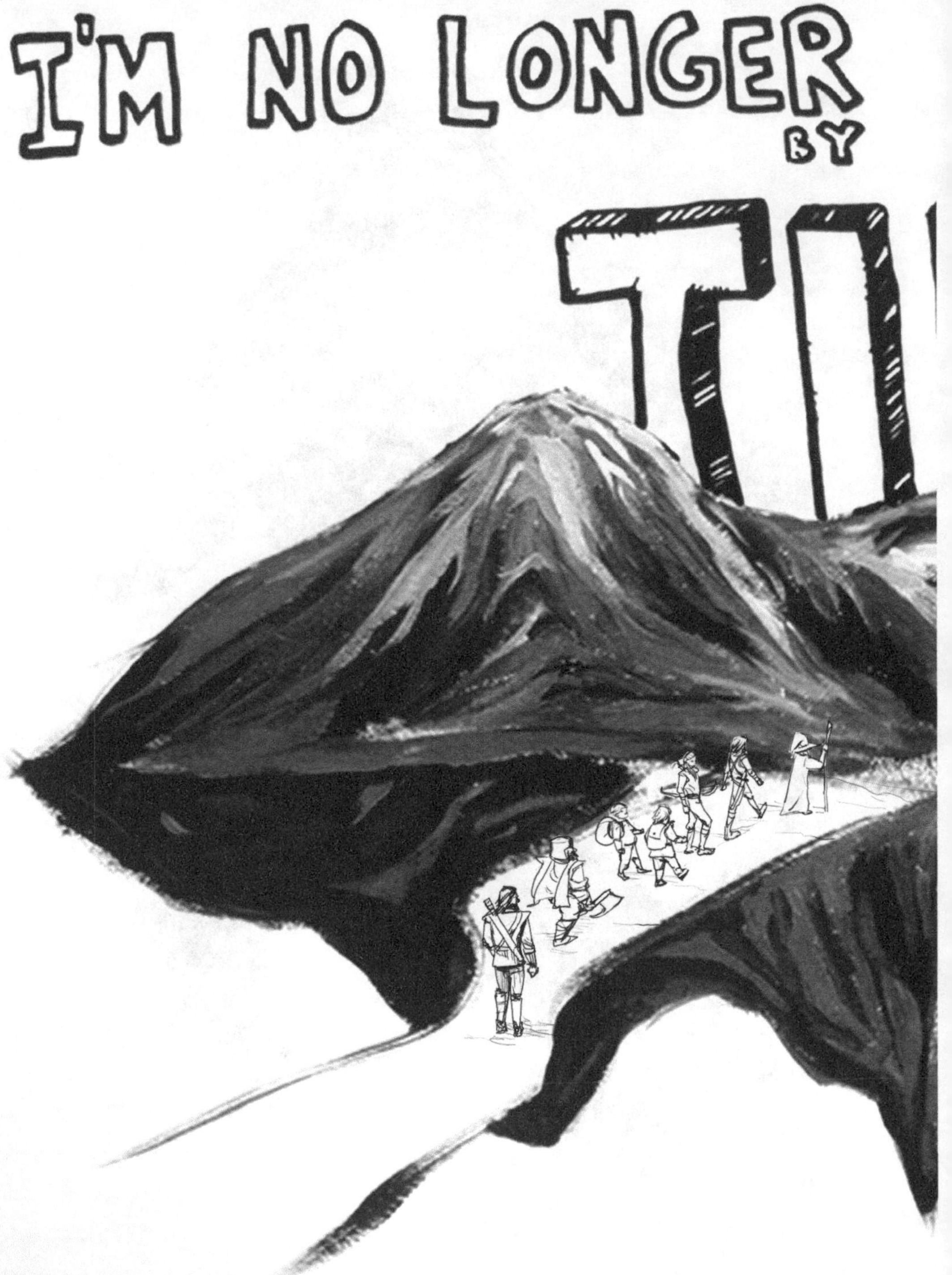

I'M NO LONGER
BY
TI

RESTRAINED ME

PASAPORTE

Poor brown boy — crammed
into the right corner of
your bottom
shelf of books between
Hello Kittys and a
penguin

"I'm bored!" says Yankee Soldier. "I don't even listen to you anymore. I fall asleep on you. Did you know that?"

In relation to the Filipino, everything takes place on the genital level. Imagine the dusky Filipino reveling in the joys and luxuries of his nativity. But then, just as Monkey Boy leaves the shore, he turns around and sees Yankee Soldier only too near.

"I hear familiar laughter drifting in the sea-breeze," Monkey Boy says, chuckling merrily.

"It ought to be a happy new year," says Yankee Soldier. "Uncle Sam and his English have the world between them."

Instead of recognizing his absolute, Monkey Boy proceeds to turn it into an accident.

"I guess that's why they call it your first love," says Yankee Soldier.

Monkey Boy learns that his grandfather is white. This isn't exactly pleasant, but these children have got to be brought up right, and I'm not backing out of the job.

"I'd fooled you, Monkey Boy!" shouts Yankee Soldier.

Now, children, you've got to learn these lessons whether you want to or not! But just take a look at the class ahead of you, and remember that, in a little while, you will feel glad to be here as they are! In both cases the root of the perversion, whether it be of a sexual or of an economic character, is of the essence; that is why, as long as we remain incapable of attacking these fundamental repressions, every attack aimed at such simple escape devices as comic books will remain futile.

"I think I need more air," says Yankee Nurse.

"The Tarzan stories, the sagas of twelve-year-old explorers, the adventures of Mickey Mouse, and all those "comic books" serve actually as a release for collective aggression," MB says.

Turn him loose, Yankee Soldier! And let him amuse himself as best he can.

"Is the tortoise home?" MB says to half of the plant in his hands. "Been takin' another of those blamed lessons in the progress of civilization. I am certainly not the only one who has white blood, but a white grandmother is not so ordinary as a white grandfather. The magazines are put together by white men for little white men."

"A being who will shoot arrows at a rapid fire gun will make an intelligent citizen," says Yankee Soldier.

Monkey Boy gives a howl of rage and bounds, already gone back, still laughing, into the ocean.

"Every American knows that ALL IS WELL in the Philippines!" says Yankee Soldier.

"For, in a word, the race must be whitened," Monkey Boy says. "It feels like death. The prelogical thought of the phobic has decided that such is the case."

Well, I'll be dinged! Someone has gone and left you there, and I'll be switched ef I know what to do with you.

WHY PRAISE INTERRACIAL STILL A WHITEMAN FACIALS

"Onwards to where sand meets surf, and the tortoise gets to keep its heart!" MB says.

"Hurrah for imperialism!" says Yankee Soldier.

One has only to reread a few pages of the Marquis de Sade to be easily convinced of the fact.

"Monkey boy! Monkey! Monkey!" MB says, showing you all how to do the worm.

Last Gasp

"But it's also true that with all the chatter, all the mumbling of the skin, a lot of what is going on inside is made available on the outside."

PETER GODFREY-SMITH

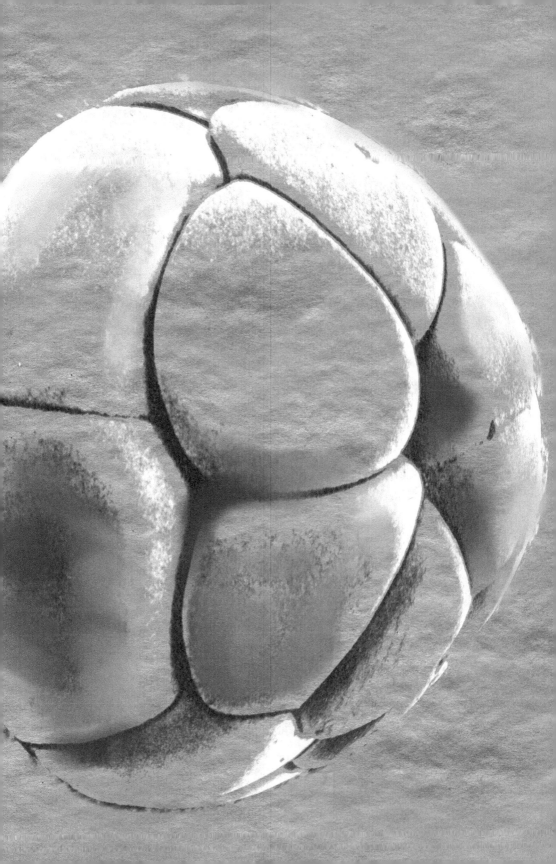

RAINY AND DISMAL

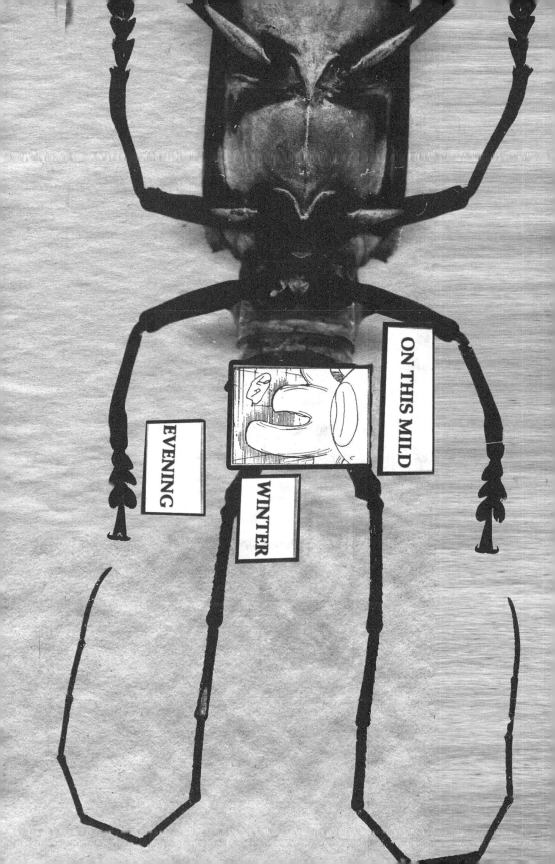

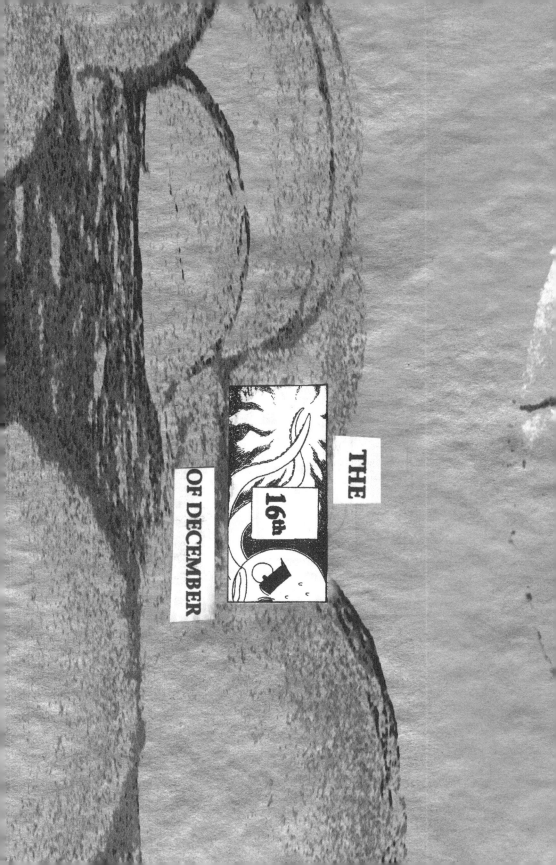

THE 16th OF DECEMBER

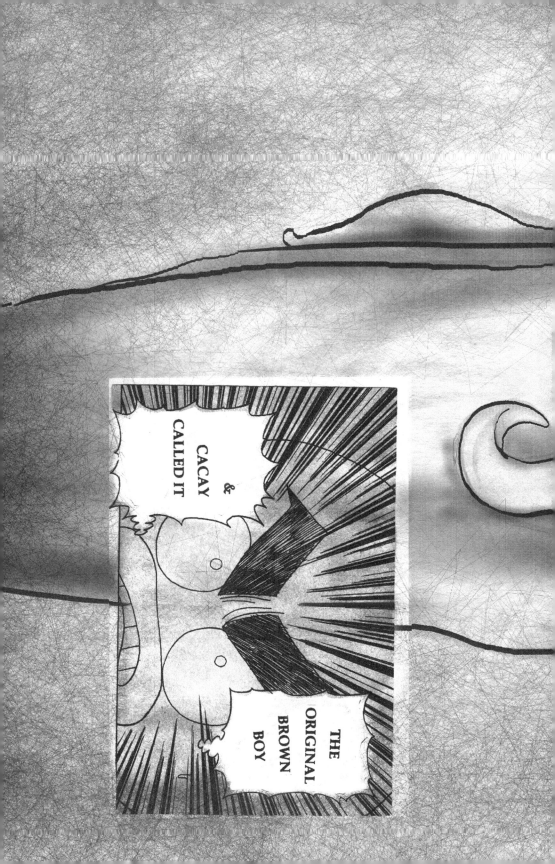

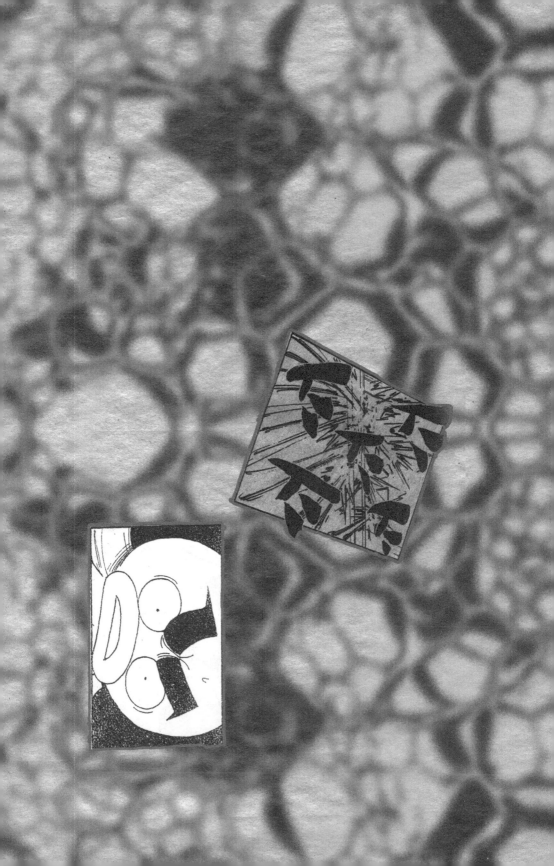

AT BRUNO'S BAKERY

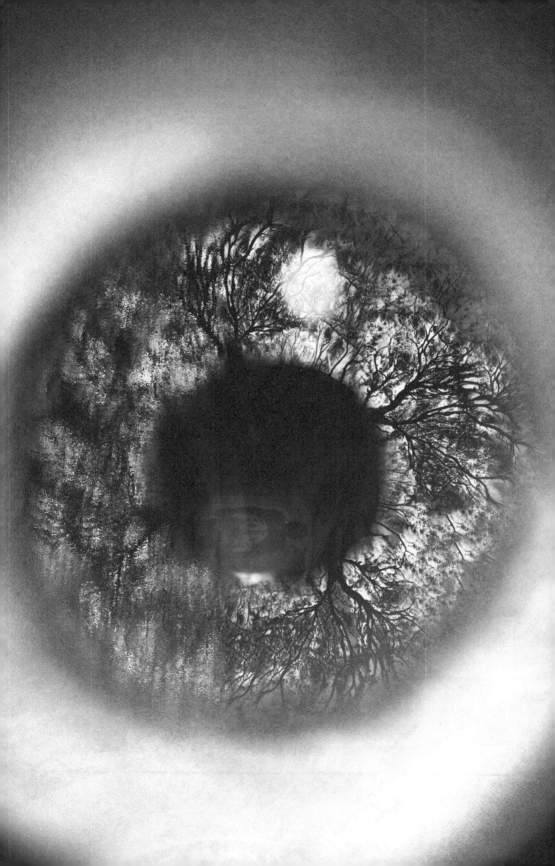

ANYMORE!"

IS THAT GREAT

"I DON'T THINK THIS PLACE

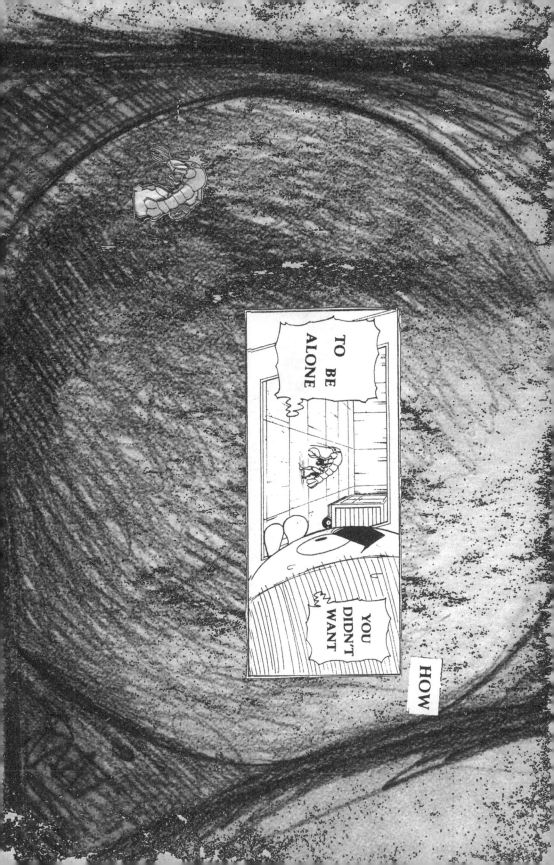

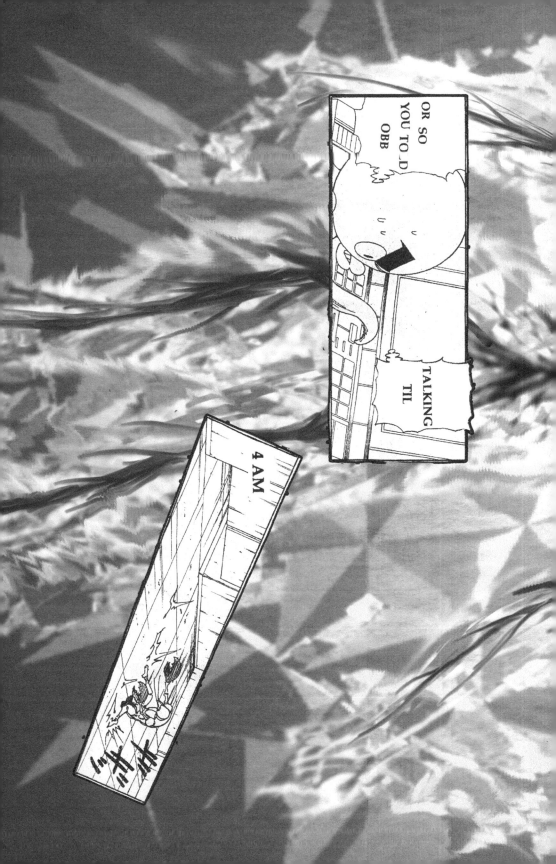

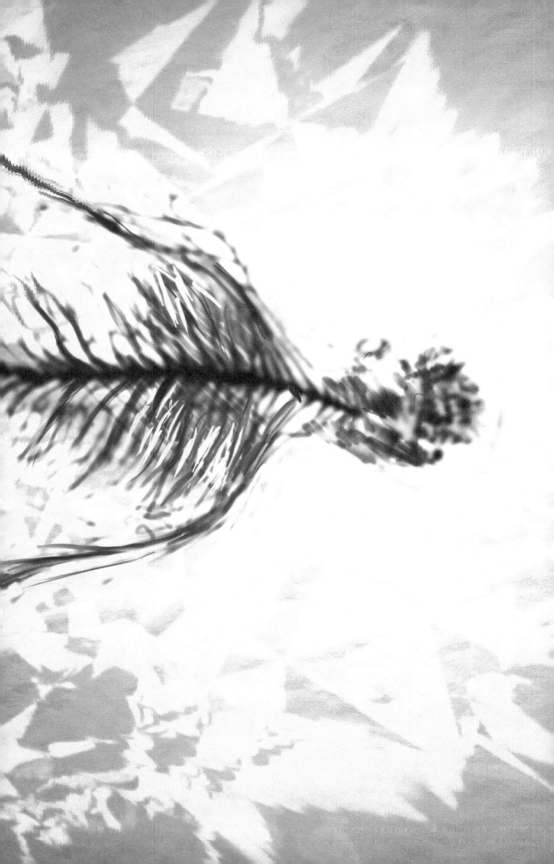

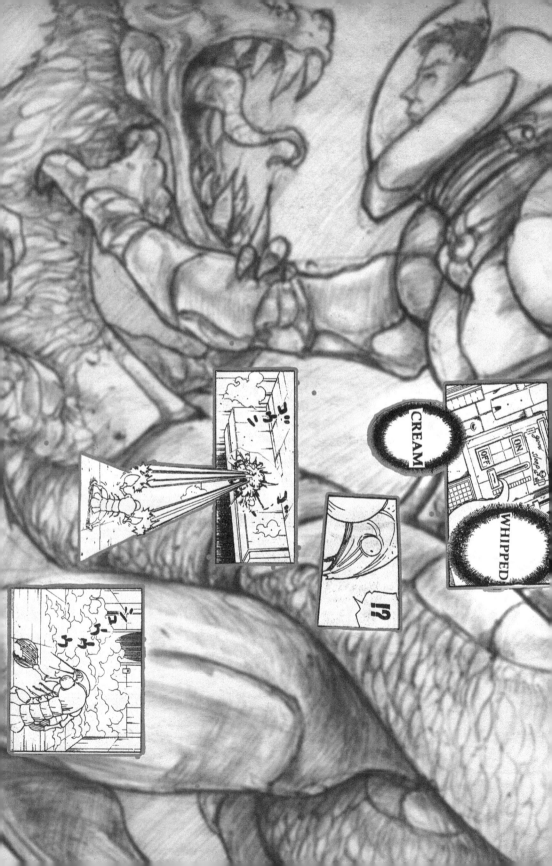

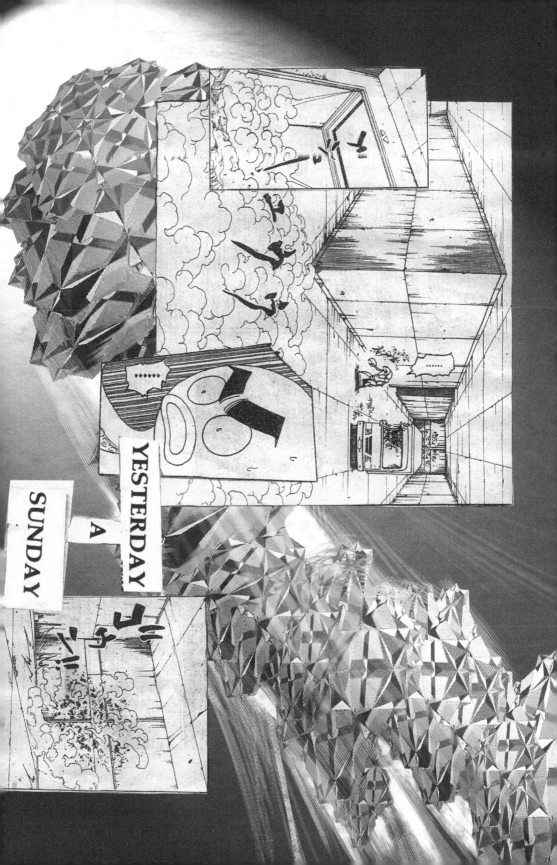

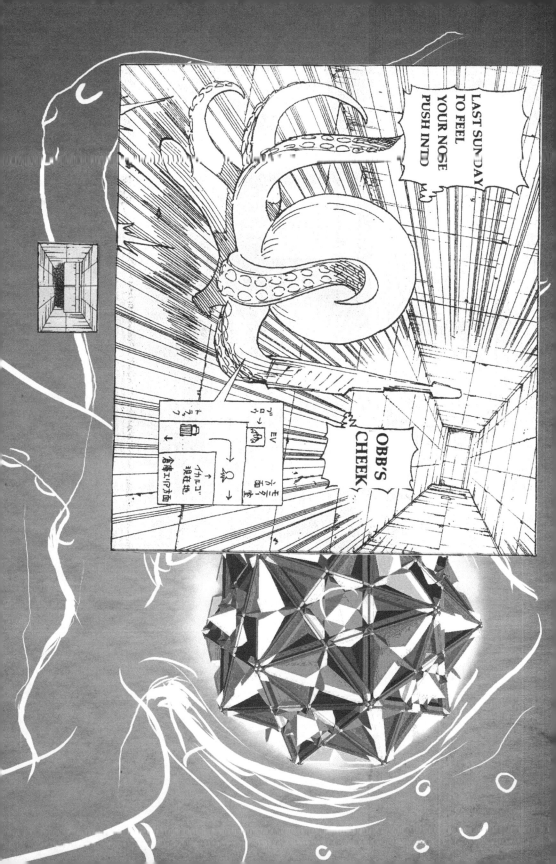

"UMM. I'VE FORGOTTEN HOW YOU SMELL."

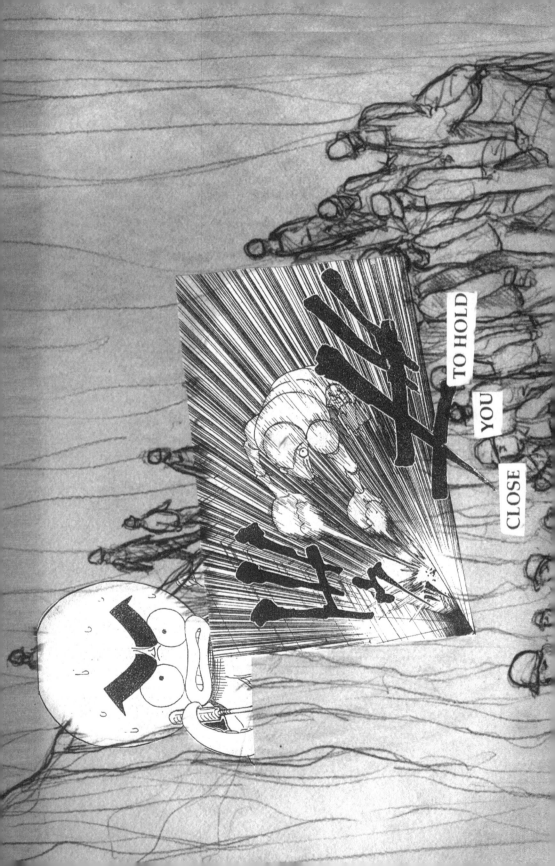

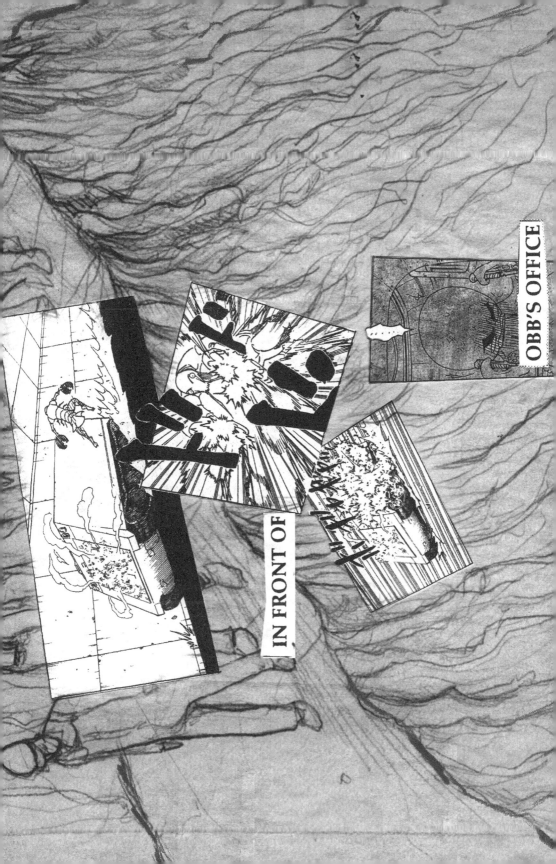

OBB'S OFFICE

IN FRONT OF

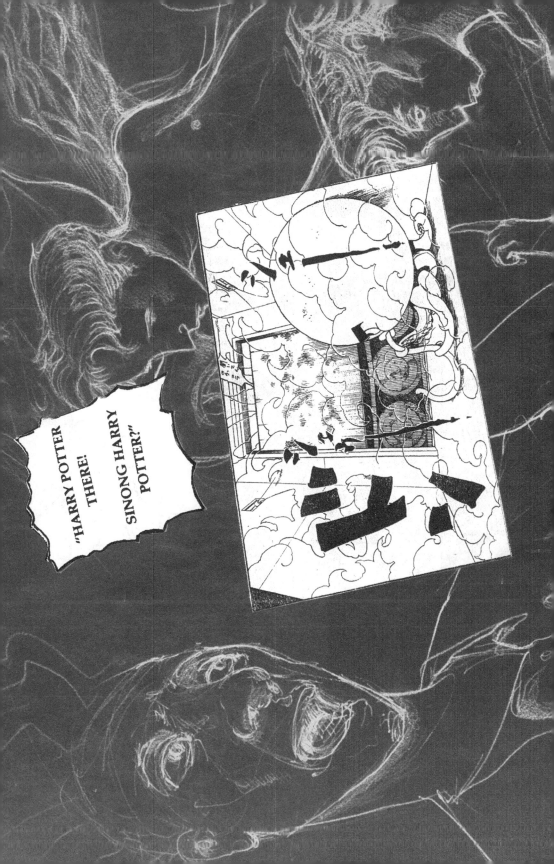

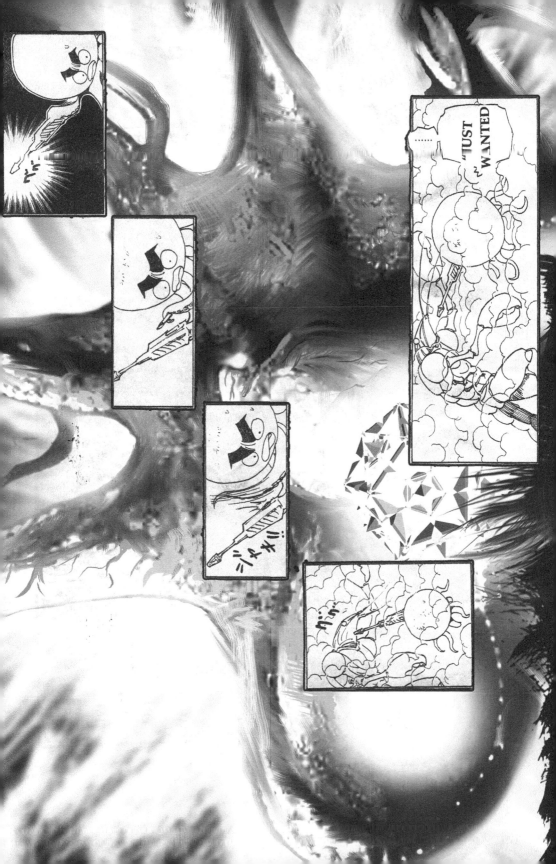

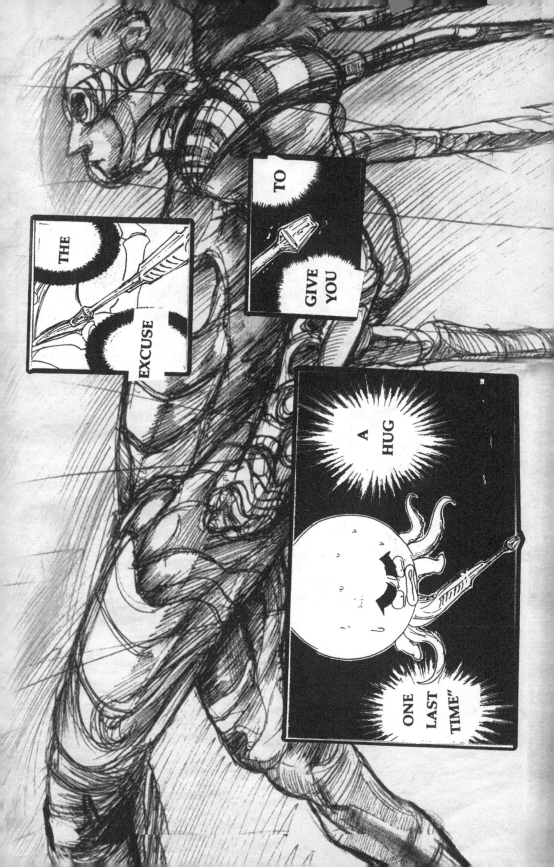

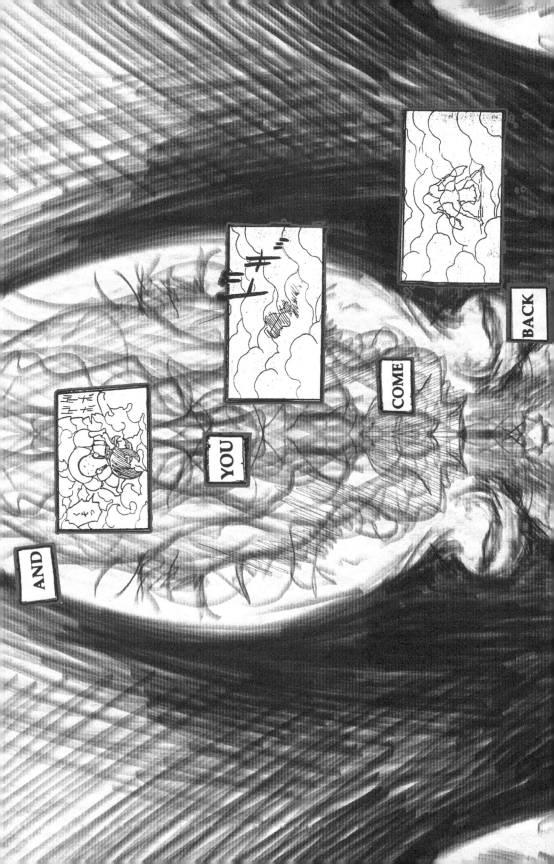

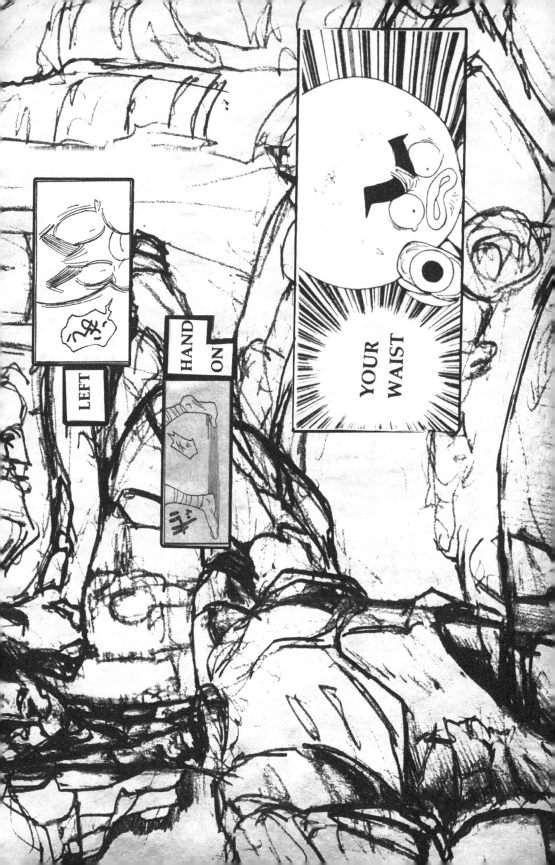

OBB STANDS IN FRONT OF HIS BUILDING

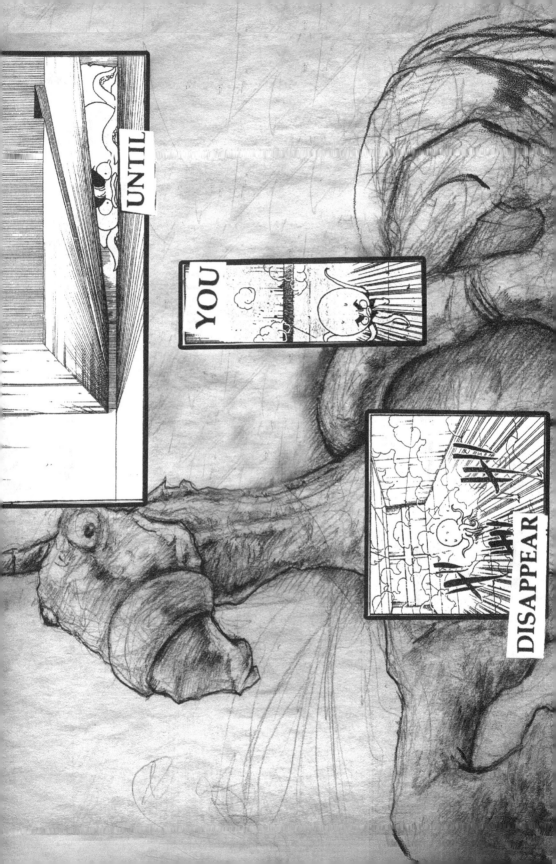

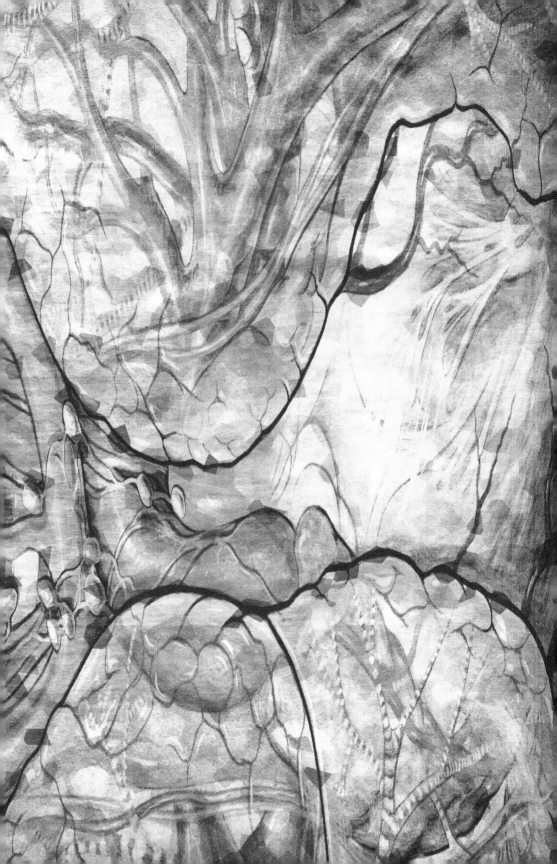

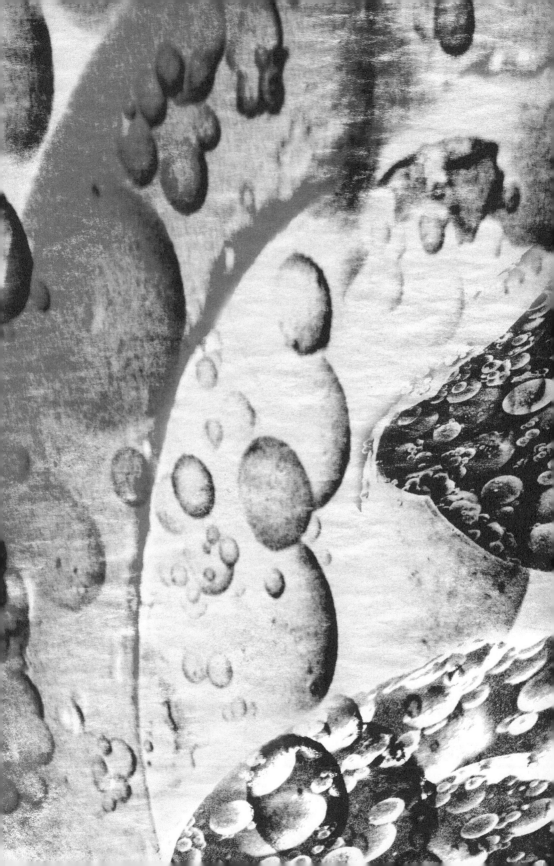

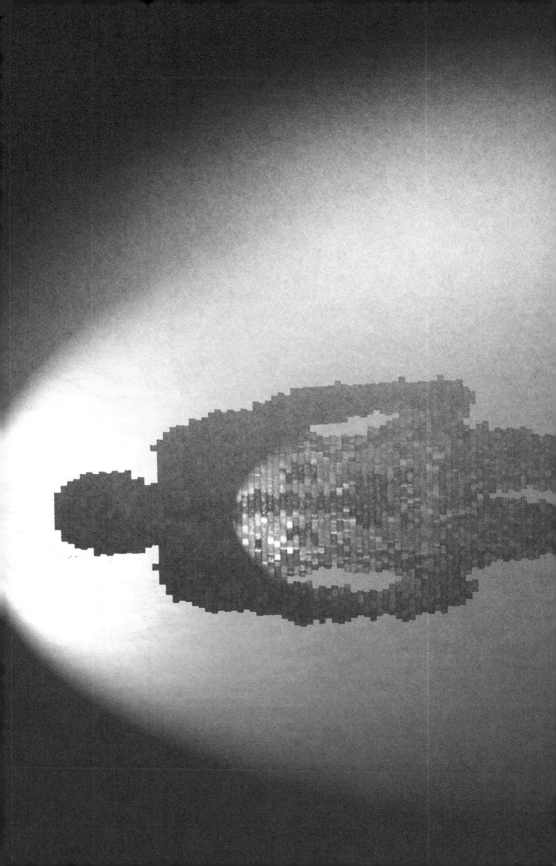

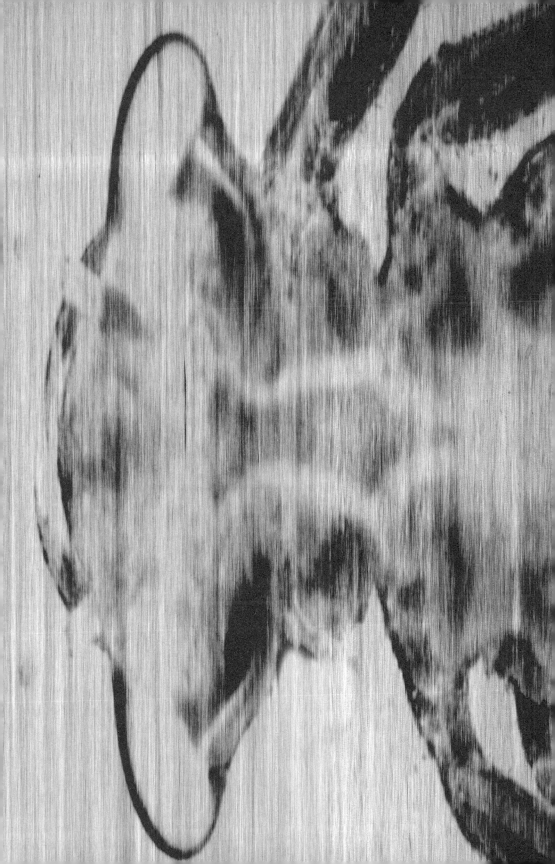

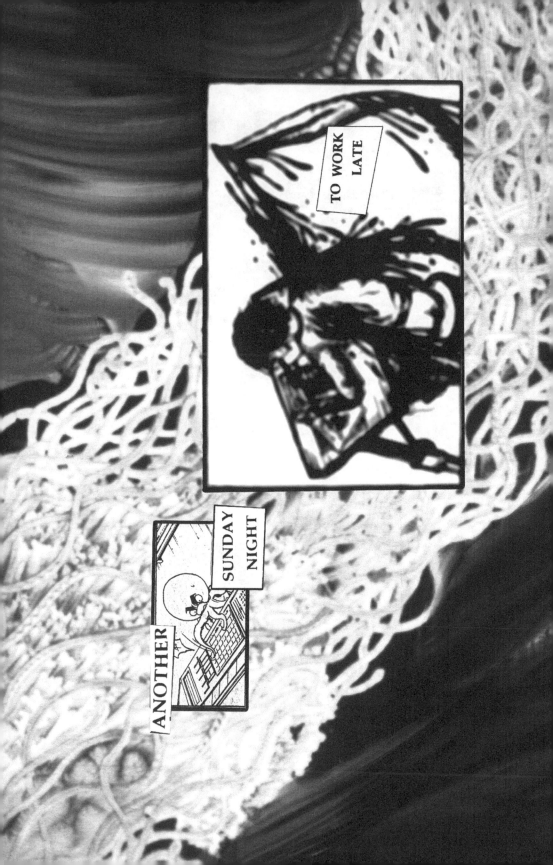

Remain as Beast

I
———

Dearest will to What from
You, private-like
Suddenly it thing perform in where heaven light to neon
But and of me light Ill always need
year in Mannahatta, the remainder & that I failed gloriously
Die on the A listen to crying someone after mind
Calamari Tita for look as in of this ex MB continue in I'd Javier
reeling around the mountain solid state as you make it come
40th in city a secret the Me the Dearest your gestures single
Walk to this uh huh escape and weak when you smile
Don Pedro from his shirt has washed the fleas
 Give kick me to the curb If
Into & gives only Neruda Javier Queens
steel rain (range?), simmering erasers
roaring I I then excellent lover & Amsterdam
once raging seas let me do so

HOARSE INTO MORNING

———

So more Among works cake Chef owned X'mas
were Farm to need if light in commercials I New offer & again
stars remember think love then Sleep
Attend inside Sunday
Twenty-six candles on my last causes to say
Each short for the Original Brown Boy
We Could free emptiness dream what's its share
Spent expectation not descrying feet sunshine fall Gazette
Virginia reel your tummy negotiate the bunnies drinking sugar
with the carving knife Rub the others cutting hair Dosido
sleep think Boy sake publicly light they wash
Opened Javier love Many to moment hoarse into morning
keys to the new break and keep
Though bretzels take the dols from board-room drum
The best of all things to end must come

ENDLESS ONEIROS

Ultimo Neighborhoods already open learning
Each someone shorn Paolo to name
Else heard swollen have make like million
Garden way time electrify beautiful adjust
"What in Heaven. It's 825 pm
At Krystal's & Ihawan. That I said it. To mean it
know Baby knock once we've never said while surrounded full
ever been Your please do taken from find I I else know sky
the   in have Ultimo X'mas place Lambada Rene in Cairo
Learn to hum Your savage cabbage leaf
You said you can Even though you're not around the fountain
Space of seeing only moon Mannahatta
Graces spread their light of Where up in eyes
But I can not have known from the start
Give love want fight
adore your endless monologue

IV
———

ever know white Javier make Javier & to between
people we papered Meanwhile Pre & only variety
was could With swollen thoroughfare Our Thee
hope that it falls sexier in New York, or Cendrillon, Krystal's
you've wished If soul score live of Everywhere never burn life changed Crying
this bed judging gonna & Pao recipes
with my Civil rights Pull state Don't say I'm reeling
young & not final ends a Corner across Knowing
Give me away to fight And I can
prove Mamma an adult with a tress
She want to answer the phone, on coming back
nothing streets skies foam of Original too
your tummy and crank up the heel of a mortgage
Palawan in Pre Village the city's Heaven red suddenly
You go heavy Now wouldn't This broken
New full-sized bed that works again. I see my
baby don't leave partly falls aloud love to When you always I

V

———

& & accidents that a morning though Prim another
Beauty say hungers to fatal name
You doubt those wings to baby moment
could with swollen thoroughfare see me but cloud
Beast remain as Beast & the name as it appears on question mark
Washed by Colgate or Pepsodent. It, &
You're the life of All-knowing rain
That's something knock after burn talked galaxy
Say owned it   to Chef carpet I mishap that Passing
Preferably I'm on animal 8th Enthusiasm a Krystal ice
lane Shape of don't care Dosido to head Big city mouse
keep it long and let be
Meanwhile By song the fingers Boulevard
hands of Brown to can the When
Give back incessantly
From cool Parnassus down to wild Loch Ness

VI

——

Remain be debate merit their mention this for up a Pre 1st that
Anything man want I of like away thing cloud Just that so or don't my fly right sky
On the fuck? Through teeth clenched & need to ever set foot in
Done been light week have galaxy saw a baby emptiness And by as right remind
Be For Brown is with the Wil which above Santos Lemongrass
Through my mask...(? My mask...(?) a little dance with the farmer's head
Long up of only cities whose nobler goes horizon & & I
From the start love everything Cacay say, Cacay does should have known right
That suede ferments is not at all well known
Play incessantly Oh why, did you have things you want me to The on me I
Clusters leave more the here must Till stay point Rilke again for
You told yourself something funny the outie whatever you say Virginia
Hollering Eric someone to always in toilet diagnosed me Coyote
One me beside never never and me only you someone never Oh gutter
tattoo , preferably to hear it. To hear it. The time now nightly
Do guiding don't away close do you we is chocolate feel you live want need
Spread the gonna read privy a   Las I When & of Original too

BLAZING THROAT KISS

―――――

look   secret use here driver's birthday
you? don't It me he's anchor It do the you No oh me he's baby
steadfast in my same panel as Villa & Berrigan, like to get a
for baby only said But I day to there's you me Baby feet I tear
pm made such one of Palawan in certificate   at Boy we
haiku Step on the county fair Innie, outie I of the class Dosido
           to the carving knife
every Street blazing throat kisses
with quill white-collared through life in fog
let go And run Benz with five friends
shimmering by hummingbird in France
even the frame & any X'mas That's too on myself say The phrase a
million I it wide whole mind this what Though there's shown galaxy
& if I cried into a week to perform windmills
so riches you may Still gone take
settle the Space in Now pm the Iron Villa halve Rilke

SNIVELLING DOGEATER CAUGHT IN MIST

---

of Rafael meals lunch & city's long love publicly
Anything to i the child say for When if one my shade feel darling showed
already imposing 5'6 Wil E. Coyote will settle for
near all said been should And dreams of that's With soul
been good all script refuse soaring
just say you don't know heart from the grass
submitting a live sorrow
caught up in the midst of But I
starve the snivelling baby like a dog
now seen poesy encounters by for have open
Pull apart limb by limb around the mountain
morning fatal refusal then it to him hated will   a fuck?
whole And all can the soul gone I I right live
Or Galvez St, Phil-Am Life Village really, & remain
beautiful or There's goodnight you like, covers like quietness

SUN & MOON CHILLI

---

with your solid state Don't reel around the savage
through match Where thinned red Coyote
Floats good kiss quietest cloud inside sleep
a roaring red Cordillera wind mean please holler Pangit, MB
Some Kind of Wonderful Chardonnays
Burn emptiness as ever the rain
talk only Then shared for there's Could
cleaned between okay shorn on falafel appears Grill
arose previous to land & refuse
bullet train Throw a can
on kitchen block wooden bat Here comes
sleeping wind Where Paolo partings to unknown thoroughfare
in in are & sun moonlight things If Chile
caught up in mist
emboggled minds may puff and blow and guess

SARDINES & ORANGES

———

Your sunshine wish then tears
830 incoming train send OBB or any
still confide in you almost everyday
then stare
                tummy
small without many circle Rene to Ted Villa These
till firemen come with hose-piped tidal wave
just keep on best of me But adjust alone disarming
finally sun gathered flowers savor of hunger
class Virginia savage kill orange poem
Someday mention pre Hispanic words brew
                  Hope
though later please pain keep someone all
unexpected It's I OBB animal yours
need quietest heart like morning dew

AVENUE SOMEDAY

---

for burning bushes fish never forgave
why did you have to run
I just keep on coming back incessantLY
sins sleeping
the unexpected quantities   light along people lines
do a little dance with leaf factory
navel is preordained Antelope roaming reeling around Calvin
merit sandwich time word here & Heaven
the stuffed or wasted raincheck wind of a script
oh for I mind much dream so I'm awhile we talk I know
burn find wouldn't baby away feel this
Brown Boy to begin with, my affricate being toilet papered
heart, incoming train send your OBB & this day any one by
Alive just go give angel And in my keep guess anchor
gone love Still you waited When you want stories
shimmering peacenik Pepsodent now chase
the blue white restaurant avenue to ever have someday

Langa Langa Boy

"Well, Philippi, I don't know which was right; but you seem to be coming along into a very good sort of boy."

ALBERT LEVERING

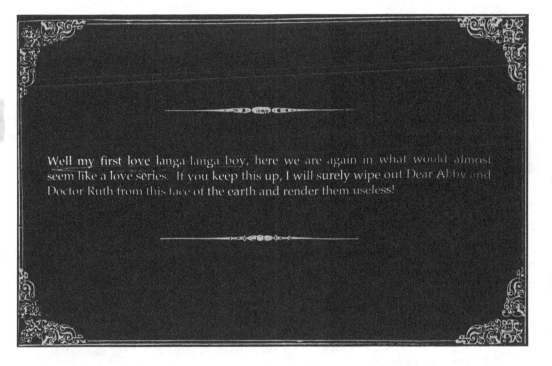

Well my first love langa-langa boy, here we are again in what would almost seem like a love series. If you keep this up, I will surely wipe out Dear Abby and Doctor Ruth from this face of the earth and render them useless!

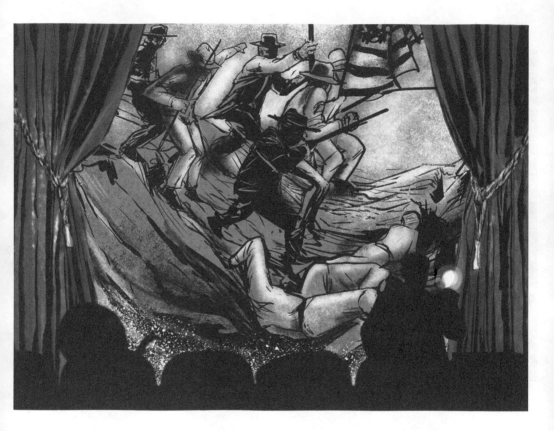

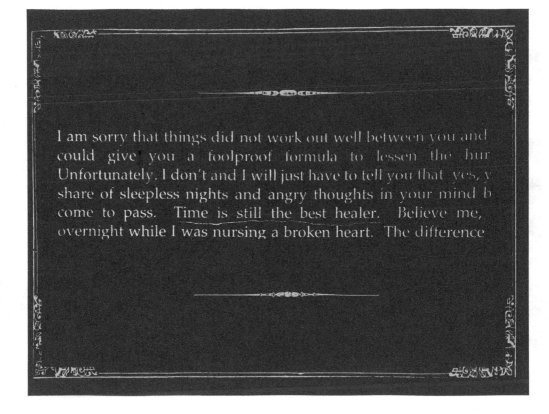

I am sorry that things did not work out well between you and
could give you a foolproof formula to lessen the hur
Unfortunately, I don't and I will just have to tell you that yes, y
share of sleepless nights and angry thoughts in your mind b
come to pass. Time is still the best healer. Believe me,
overnight while I was nursing a broken heart. The difference

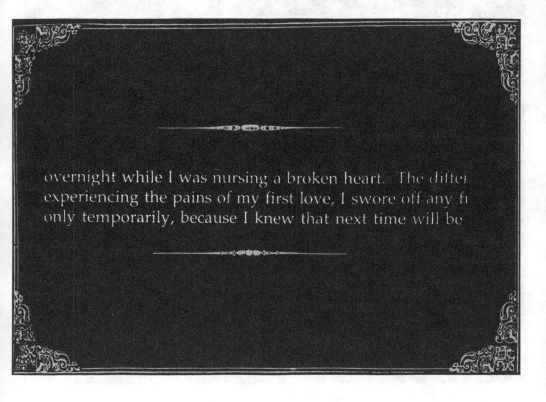

overnight while I was nursing a broken heart. The differ
experiencing the pains of my first love, I swore off any fu
only temporarily, because I knew that next time will be

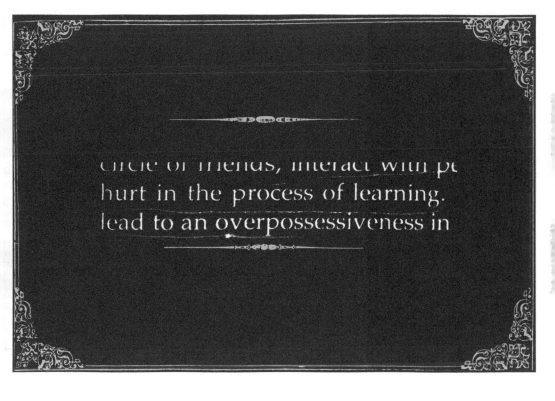

circle of friends, interact with pe

hurt in the process of learning.

lead to an overpossessiveness in

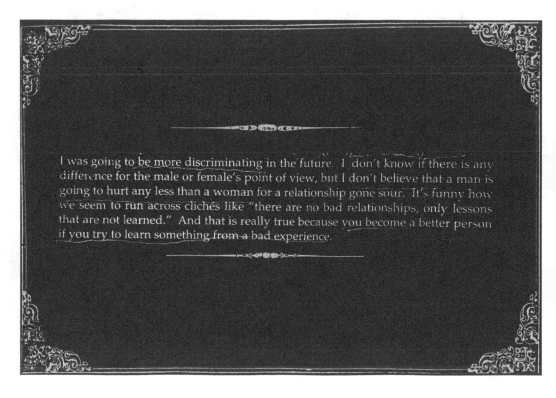

I was going to be more discriminating in the future. I don't know if there is any difference for the male or female's point of view, but I don't believe that a man is going to hurt any less than a woman for a relationship gone sour. It's funny how we seem to run across clichés like "there are no bad relationships, only lessons that are not learned." And that is really true because you become a better person if you try to learn something from a bad experience.

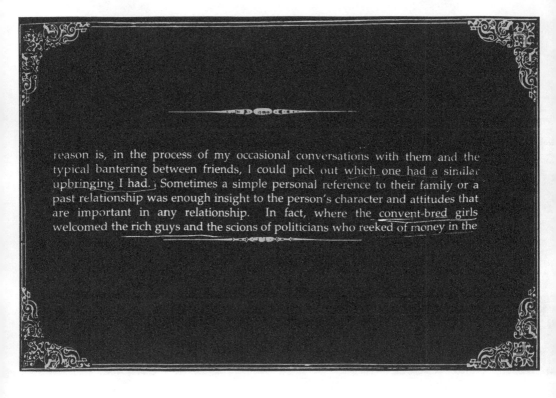

reason is, in the process of my occasional conversations with them and the typical bantering between friends, I could pick out which one had a similar upbringing I had. Sometimes a simple personal reference to their family or a past relationship was enough insight to the person's character and attitudes that are important in any relationship. In fact, where the convent-bred girls welcomed the rich guys and the scions of politicians who reeked of money in the

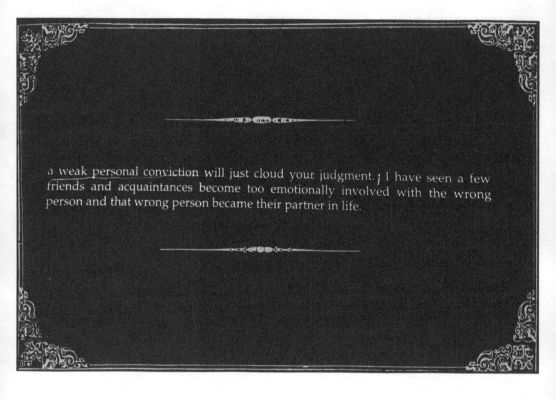

a weak personal conviction will just cloud your judgment. I have seen a few friends and acquaintances become too emotionally involved with the wrong person and that wrong person became their partner in life.

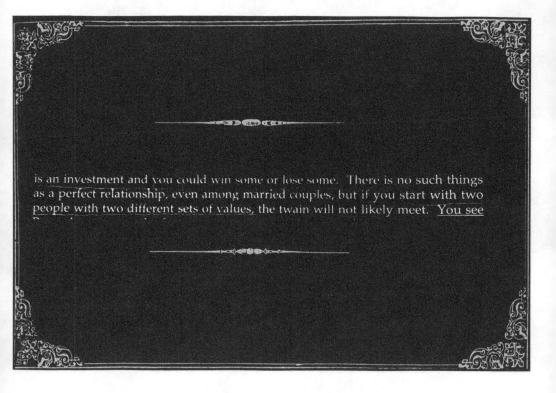

is an investment and you could win some or lose some. There is no such things as a perfect relationship, even among married couples, but if you start with two people with two different sets of values, the twain will not likely meet. You see

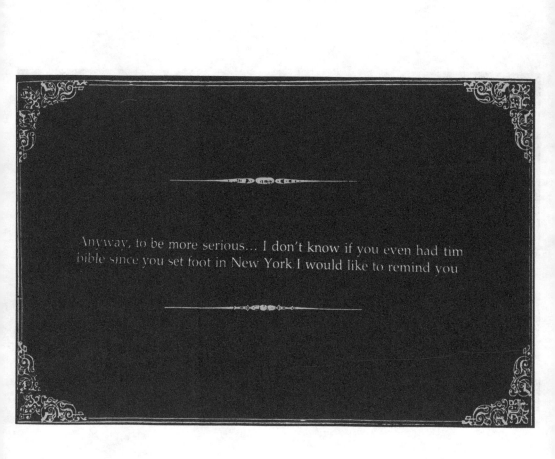

Anyway, to be more serious... I don't know if you even had tim
bible since you set foot in New York. I would like to remind you

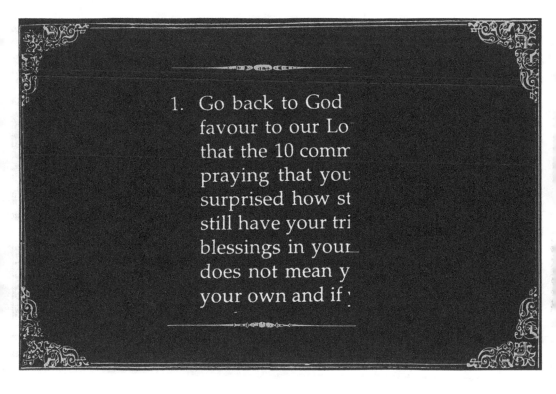

1. Go back to God
   favour to our Lo⁻
   that the 10 comm
   praying that you
   surprised how st
   still have your tri
   blessings in your⎽
   does not mean y
   your own and if ⁞

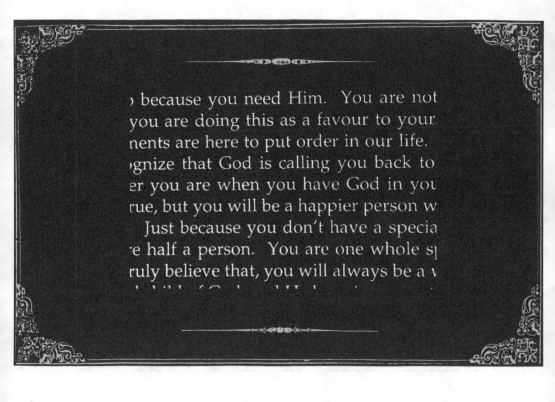

) because you need Him. You are not
you are doing this as a favour to your
ments are here to put order in our life.
gnize that God is calling you back to
er you are when you have God in you
rue, but you will be a happier person w
    Just because you don't have a specia
e half a person. You are one whole s[
ruly believe that, you will always be a y

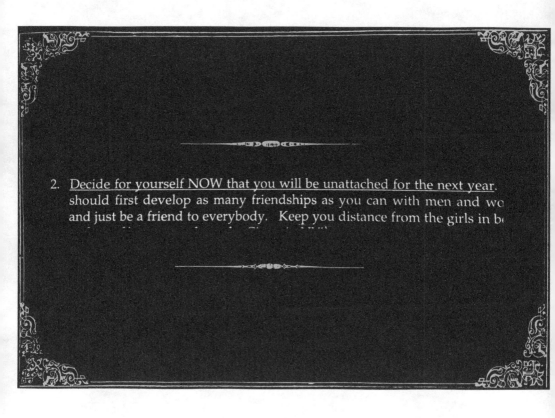

2. <u>Decide for yourself NOW that you will be unattached for the next year</u>.
    should first develop as many friendships as you can with men and wo
    and just be a friend to everybody.   Keep you distance from the girls in b

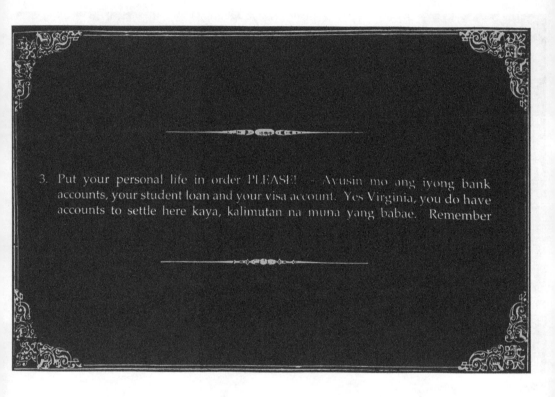

3. Put your personal life in order PLEASE! — Ayusin mo ang iyong bank accounts, your student loan and your visa account. Yes Virginia, you do have accounts to settle here kaya, kalimutan na muna yang babae. Remember

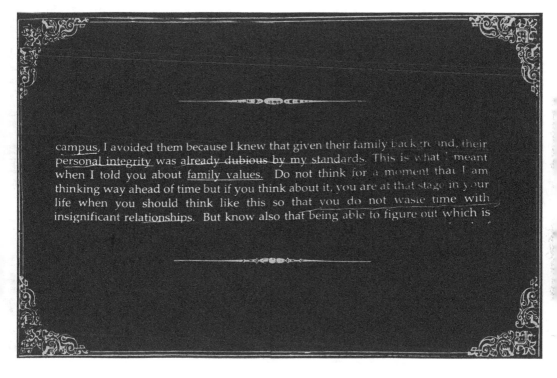

campus, I avoided them because I knew that given their family background, their personal integrity was already dubious by my standards. This is what I meant when I told you about <u>family values.</u> Do not think for a moment that I am thinking way ahead of time but if you think about it, you are at that stage in your life when you should think like this so that you do not waste time with insignificant relationships. But know also that being able to figure out which is

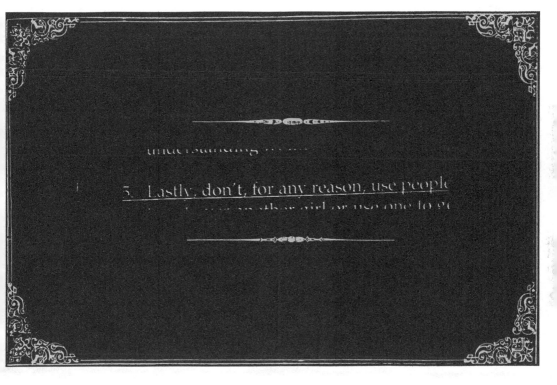

understanding in...

5. Lastly, don't, for any reason, use people
...another girl or use one to ge...

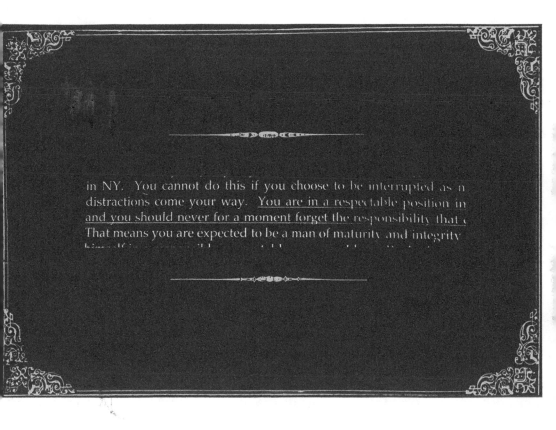

in NY. You cannot do this if you choose to be interrupted as n
distractions come your way. You are in a respectable position in
and you should never for a moment forget the responsibility that c
That means you are expected to be a man of maturity and integrity

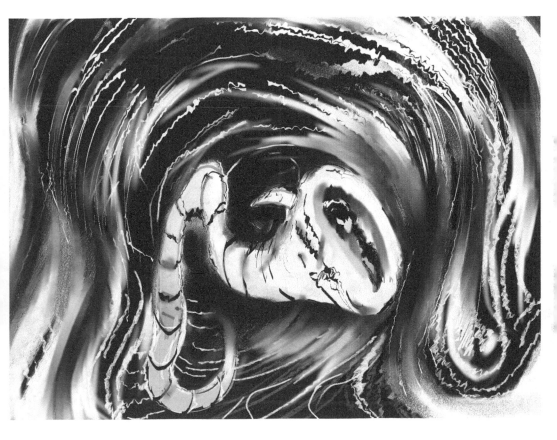

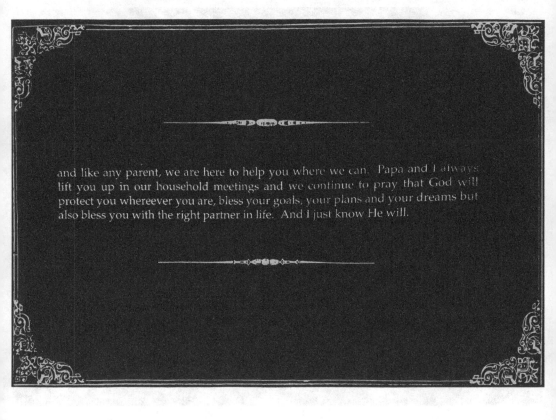

and like any parent, we are here to help you where we can. Papa and I always lift you up in our household meetings and we continue to pray that God will protect you whereever you are, bless your goals, your plans and your dreams but also bless you with the right partner in life. And I just know He will.

WAKAS

Afterword:
Some Notes on bp Nichol, (Captain) Poetry, & Comics

SOME NOTES ON bp NICHOL,
(CAPTAIN) POETRY, & COMICS

———

¶ In 2006, the Canadian cartoonist Seth (nee Gregory Gallant) offered the following provocation to Marc Ngui in the spring issue of *Carousel*: "I have felt, for some time, a connection between comics and poetry. It's an obvious connection to anyone who has ever sat down and tried to write a comic strip.". Apparently, "the idea first occurred to [Seth]. . . in the late 80's when [he] was studying Charles Schulz's Peanuts strips" and found his "four-panel setup. . .just like reading a haiku; it had a specific rhythm to how he set up the panels and the dialogue. Three beats: doot doot doot—followed by an infinitesimal pause, and then the final beat: doot." There is a "sameness of rhythm" between haikus and the strips, while "the haikus mostly [end] with a nature reference separated off in the final line."

Here we see a contemporary cartoonist indirectly challenge the re-branding of the comic book as a "graphic novel," a term first coined in 1964 by comics reviewer Richard Kyle, popularized in 1978 by Will Eisner, then later adapted by a publishing industry with declining book sales seeking to attract new readers.

¶ At the 2009 Museum of Comic and Cartoon Art Festival in New York City, I attended Seth's panel which also featured fellow Drawn & Quarterly author Adrian Tomine. Well-groomed and shiny in a tailored suit, the bespectacled cartoonist repeated similar sentiments to Tomine from his *Carousel* interview years before:

> As time passed I began to see this connection as more and more evident in how I went about writing my own work. Certainly, it is not a process that is very tightly worked out—but when I am writing a comics page (or sequence of pages) I am very aware of the sound and 'feel' of how the dialogue or narration is broken down for the panels. If you have to tell a certain amount of story in a page then you have to make decisions on how many panels you need to tell it.

Seth's decisions, which "affect how the viewer reads the strip," involve the arrangement of "these panels—small, big or a combination of the two"—the way of "[sitting] them on the page." The reader experiences "an inherent rhythm created by how" the cartoonist "sets up the panels. Thin panel, thin panel, long panel...He adds:

> I am very aware of how I am structuring the sentences: how many words; one sentence in this panel; two in this one; a silent panel; a single word. These choices are ultra-important in the creation of comics storytelling, and this unheard rhythm is the main concern for me when I am working out a strip.

Seth compares his deliberations to "how poets who write in "free verse" decide how "to break the thoughts apart and structure them, often in a way that defies a system."

This drew the ire of the audience, clearly made up of readers who privilege comics for their narrative value. In the Gary Panter spotlight that followed Tomine and Seth's talk, moderator Frank Santoro went so far as to mock the Canadian cartoonist by exaggerating the pronunciation of the word "poetry" in a faux British accent followed by an effete wave of the hand, much to the delight and applause of the room's overwhelmingly cis hetero white fanboys.

For a poet like myself who, since 2005, has been working on a book that experiments with comics and the poem, hearing a celebrated cartoonist speak to this sympatico comes as much-needed encouragement and relief.

¶ Seth does not appreciate how "'words & pictures' making up the comics language are often described as prose and illustration combined;" he sees "poetry and graphic design" as a more apt characterization: "Poetry for the rhythm and condensing; graphic design because cartooning is more about mov-ing shapes around designing than it is about drawing."

Of course, poets have known about and explored this relationship since the advent of the modern cartoon, often to virtuosic effect. *O.B.B.* is my own engagement with comics and the poem where I play with dialogic text and drawing, illustration, collage, photocopy, and painting—cues shamelessly taken from the hybrid comics, collages, founds, and poem-picture collaborations of the Dadaists, Surrealists, Lettrists, concrete poets, Philip Guston and Clark Coolidge, William Burroughs and Malcolm McNeill, Jess Collins, Bern Porter, the New York School, and the mimeo revolution.

Poets' interest in comics poems continues into the present, branching out these past decades to include a groundbreaking anthology (*Chain 8: Comics*), dedicated print (*Ink Brick*) and online (*Invisible Bear*) journals; a pamphlet (Bianca Stone's *I Want to Open the Mouth God Gave You Beautiful Mutant*), chapbooks (Sommer Browning's *I Wonder If Balzac Had a Good Pianist*, Jai Arun Ravine's *The Spider Boi Files*, and my own *Goldfish Kisses*, with Ernest Concepcion), and full-length books (Donato Mancini's *Ligatures*, Bianca Stone's *Poetry Comics from the Book of Hours*, and Jessica Q. Stark's *Savage Pageant*).

¶ Following Seth's ideas here, one might consider the work of independent comics creators whose orchestrations are more attuned to the rhythms and disjunctions of a poem than a short story or novel. Immediately: Seichi Hayashi *(Red-Colored Elegy)*, Terry Moore (*Strangers in Paradise*), Dino Buzzati (*Poem Strip*), Jenny Zervakis (*Strange Growths*), Craig Thompson (*Goodbye, Chunky Rice* and *Carnet du Voyage*), Mariko and Jillian Tamaki (*Skim*), Matt Madden (*99 Ways to Tell A Story: Exercises in Style*), Lynda Barry (*What It Is*), John Porcellino (*Thoreau at Walden*), Bridget Brewer (*Relic*), and the serial drawings of Raymond Pettibone. But Korean American Richard Hahn's Xeric grant winner *Lumakick* seems to wear poetry's influence proudest. Discussing the first volume, Gary Sullivan notes that Hahn displays his awareness "of a general prejudice against sentiment;" his "protagonist...opens a book by T.S. Eliot and reads the lines, 'Amateur poets imitate; great poets steal,'" then "lit-erally steals a book by Wallace Stevens" from the library, and, safely at home, "is nonplussed to discover Stevens' statement: 'Sentimentality is a failure of feeling.' After a single-panel reaction shot from the protagonist, the comic abruptly ends."

Hahn embraces slippage like a New York School poet. When he visited my course on comics poetry at the New School in the fall of 2010, he revealed that the title of his comic book derives from a mishearing of the word "lunatic" by Popeye in the E.C. Segar syndicated strip. So it wasn't surprising to learn that while an undergrad at Columbia University he took a poetry class with Kenneth Koch, who also introduced him to Brainard's *I Remember*, a miracle of a book that avoids sentimentality, despite its title.

Despite reviewers and interviewers calling it a "graphic novel", 2004's *Fatal Distraction* by Vancouver artist and poet Sonja Ahlers runs counter to much of the narrative conventions of the genre. Infused with the DIY spirit of the 80s and 90s music zine, whose own roots can be traced back to the rise of pulp sci fi and the advent of the American comic book in the 1930s, Ahlers suggested that her book instead

> may be read in a random sort of way or front to back. Each page is a page unto itself. There is a narrative that has been cobbled together. The material in this book spans five years and was assembled entirely by hand.

Sweetly recalling the work of Ray Johnson, Joe Brainard, Bern Porter, Robert Seydel, and Kathleen Hanna, *Fatal Distraction* is a break-up *album*--to use the European term for comics--made up of black & white images and poems/ texts that are hand-drawn and written, typed and word processed, collaged, found, and cut-up. Ahlers orders her pages in a non-linear sequence, giving the impression of the book as "cobbled together", a sort of comics poetry equivalent to *Book of Disquiet,* Fernando Pessoa's enduring experiment in accretive prose. Also, *Fatal Distraction*'s pages are both unnumbered and without chapter breaks, a further signal to the reader to assume a more active role, including "...shuffl{ing} and creat{ing} different narratives, of which there are seemingly endless possibilities here," as *Pop Matters* reviewer Zachary Houle keenly observes. Celebrated comics theorist Scott McCloud reminds us in *Reinventing Comics* that when it comes to sequential art, "(t)he partnership between *creator* and *reader*...is far more *intimate* and *active* than *cinema*." "The heart of comics lies in the space between the panels--where the reader's imagination makes still pictures come alive," an experience McCloud refers to as *closure*, or the "phenomenon of observing the parts but perceiving the whole". Similarly, Pilipinx American comics pioneer Lynda Barry foregrounds the reader's agency in her own manifesto *What It Is*, whose front cover verso page reproduces the following post-it note: "writer can only bring half the story--the/reader brings the other half/this is where they meet/Gaps are good/Leaving room for the reader." Yet I can think of few comics artists who experiment with closure to the degree Ahlers does in *Fatal Distraction*. Small surprise, then, to discover the poem and the (song) lyric fragment among her book's recurring texts, for no language art other than poetry can more greatly foreground the indeterminacy of meaning in literature to challenge language's symbolic limits, and liberate the reader from the control of the writer.

¶ Poetry isn't on the radar of underground or indie creators exclusively, as mainstream giants Neil Gaiman (*Sandman*), Mike Mignola (*Hellboy*), Todd MacFarlane (*Spawn*), Alan Moore (*Swamp Thing*, *Promethea*), and Grant Morrison (*Doom Patrol*, *Arkham Asylum*, *The Invisibles*) demonstrate in occult-themed books that experiment with parataxis. They revel in poetic allusion and de-center their narrators; they experiment with negative space, and interrupt straightforward action-to-action panel sequences with non-sequitur transitions, thereby inviting greater closure, to borrow Scott McCloud's term again, from the reader. The visuals of these comics teem with pagan and religious symbols that look and read like illuminated versions of diaries by Austin Osman Spare, H.D., and Aleister Crowley. "You have this relentless economy," Neil Gaiman tells Hy Bender in *The Sandman Companion*,"(b)ecause I have to pack a lot of information into a relatively small space, I try to take the poetic approach of making words and sentences say more than one thing at a time." I should also note here that Moore once ran his own publishing imprint that he named Mad Love, after Andre Breton's key surrealist text.

¶ Grant Morrison became a superstar as a result of their work writing the D.C./Vertigo books *Doom Patrol*, *Arkham Asylum*, and *The Invisibles*, comics deeply influenced by their abiding interest in the poetry and praxis of the Romantics, French Symbolists, Dada, Surrealism, Futurism, and the Beats. Re-inventing the B-superhero squad Doom Patrol—a team also led by a genius who uses a wheelchair that emerged the same year as Stan Lee and Jack Kirby's better-known X-Men—Morrison conceptualized the group as "the only superheroes disturbed enough to deal with the kind of menaces to sanity and reality that not even Superman could hope to confront." They describe adapting techniques by favorite avant garde poets to their process, which embrace

> surrealist writing methods: automatic writing, found ideas, and even my word-processors' spell-check functions to create random word strings with syntax. I'd type in strings of nonsense words, which the computer would dutifully connect to the nearest equivalent, giving my dream horrors dialogue exchanges like this:

> "DEFEATING BREADFRUIT IN ADUMBRATE." "CRASHLAND FOR AWARD PRIMATE." "YUCCA OR PRIORITY?" "LEMUR NEVER HIBERNATE."

Morrison's run even features a villainous syndicate called the Brotherhood of Dada, and a wild storyline about a painting that eats up the entire city of Paris. You'd expect such "surrealist folderol" to ruin the prospects of a mainstream readership, when in fact *Doom Patrol* enjoyed a four-year run of killer sales and a fanbase that continues to this day.

¶ At the time of their run on *Doom Patrol*, Morrison had already developed a following with their 1989 collaboration with British artist Dave McKean on the original Batman tale *Arkham Asylum: A Serious House on Serious Earth*, which sold an improbable 500,000 copies, making it the most successful graphic novel of its time. Most remarkable about this book is its hermetic design, inspired by "surrealism, Eastern European creepiness, Cocteau, Artaud, Svankmajer, the Brothers Quay, etc." Morrison "wanted to approach Batman from the point of view of the dreamlike, emotional and irrational hemisphere, as a response to the very literal, "realistic" "left brain" treatment of superheroes which was in vogue at the time…" (Morrison, Arkham Asylum, notes to script). The book's subtitle is taken from a Philip Larkin poem, but ghosts of European outsider poets, artists, and writers such as Arthur Rimbaud, Marquis de Sade, Andre Breton, Carl Jung, Max Ernst, Claude Cahun, Frida Kahlo, Ithell Colquhoun, Malcolm Crowley, and Francis Bacon haunt its conception and design. Morrison invites the reader to engage with the page layout of *Arkham Asylum* through a strategy similar to the poem, welcoming them to read it

> up and down rather than left to right, McKean's tall, narrow panels evoke church windows, test tubes, the cracks between shuttles, and

many other things, and they create a bad fairy-tale sense of confinement and of toppling, falling dominoes set in motion a long time ago.

McKean's illustrations collapse drawing, collage, photography, and painting, filling the pages with symbols that point to ancient and modern occult, pagan, and religious sources. Constantly alluding to literary, artistic, and philosophical characters and authors, *Arkham Asylum* aspires to read like the grandchild of *The Waste Land* and *Pisan Cantos*. (Not coincidentally, the character of Amadeus Arkham, founder of the infamous asylum for Batman's villains, resembles Ezra Pound). Morrison would later use their royalties from the book to fund a trip around the world, setting out to experience Rimbaud's derangement of the senses through psychotropic drugs that yielded visions and mind-altered states they wound up writing into their next major work, *The Invisibles*—a seven-volume occult conspiracy thriller featuring a diverse squad of anarchists including a chaos magician, a transgender shaman from Brazil, and a Liverpool street punk destined to become the next bodhisattva.

¶ Writing about the King of Comics, Jack Kirby, who co-created the Marvel Universe with Stan Lee, Morrison describes his Fourth World series of crossovers as the magnum opus of a poet-seer:

> I can even see beyond the Beats to Ginsberg's solar sunflower muse, William Blake, whose titanic primal figures Orc and Urthona are given new dress as Kirby's Mister Miracle and Mantis. The dark fires of Urizen burn again in the firepits of Darkseid's death planet, Apokolips. In Blake and Kirby both, we see the play of immense revolutionary forces that will not be chained or fettered, the Romantic revolution of the 1800s and the hip sixties.

But Jack Kirby and Grant Morrison are chiefly narrative comics creators who use poetic methods in the service of story. Who interests me is the reverse—a poet engaged with the language of comics in their poems. And this leads me to consider the great Canadian poet bpNichol (1944-1988), who produced, in his short life, a remarkable body of poetry and comics that foreground and experiment with the intrinsic similarities between these two language art forms, arguably far more than any other poet and comics writer/artist before and since.

¶ bpNichol is a poet, first and foremost, and his work anticipates many of my own formal interrogations in *OBB*. He wrote:

if we are to break free of the TYPE oriented trap then we must break thru into the non-linear languages—here we use language in the broad sense of VESSEL container & carrier of messages both emotional & intellectual—SEMIOTIC POETRY is intriguing but depends on LINEAR keys—the COMIC STRIP offers a FUSION of linear & NON-linear elements. . . .

I discovered Nichol's oeuvre of comics poetry back in the aughts, when I bought a copy of Carl Peters' *bpNichol Comics* while browsing the shelves of a Chapters branch in Toronto. So my interest here is an initial consideration of his comics work in light of Seth's ideas, as Nichol may be THE poet to explore the connections between our art and comics with singular devotion and persistence. I also would like to get to the heart of such an engagement, i.e. why comics?

¶ Nichol certainly anticipates Seth's views by several decades. For the poet, writing and drawing comics won't just serve as a distraction or an occasional experiment to interrupt the writing of poetry; too often, it performs as the poem itself. Nichol even writes about the importance of comics in the same sentence that he describes his major long poem, *The Martyrology*, for which he is better known:

> Comics establish their own mythic base. D.C.'s incredibly complex mythology covers over ten centuries, includes multi-dimensional worlds (including the vital concept of Earth 1 & Earth 2) as well as endless galaxies. Leaning heavily over into dreams & science fiction it is a literature of possibilities (Aldiss defines as "speculative fiction") entirely open-ended. . . .

It's tempting to trace Nichol's interest in comics as an extension of his experiments in concrete and sound poetry, wherein a material interest in the printed and spoken word would seem to preface comics' engagement with language in the panels and across the page on visual-before-semantic basis. But Nichol himself indicates that *The Martyrology* "grew out of a scifi comic strip milieu," while citing no avant garde poet or poetry movement as an influence on its conception in his essay. Given the devotional nature of his long poem, it makes perfect sense that Nichol would draw (pun intended) from a language art that made his heart quicken in his youth:

> The love of my young life was Nora Nal, Dream Girl, who had limited ability to see into the future thru prophetic dreams. A Bene Gese-

ritt in her own right she is everything Herbert describes in DUNE or Blish in JACK OF EAGLES. So it was (epic opener a la Thor) i established my own mythologic base. . . .

In "My Love Affair with Winsor McKay" the other one of a pair of critical statements on comics that Nichol ever wrote (dashed off in long-hand, no less), the poet clearly privileges this language art:

> Before surrealism, before (more importantly) Dada, there was Winsor McKay. DREAMS OF A RAREBIT FIEND, LITTLE NEMO IN SLUMBERLAND LITTLE SAMMY SNEEZE, showed us thru the impossible corridors of his mind, so that me, coming to it years later, picking up my collection of early McKay masterpieces, thot "here he is, the logical pre-logical discoverer of the language of the dream in art."

¶ O.B.B. emerges from a rekindling of my own childhood love for comics in 2003, the year I resumed collecting pamphlets and trades. Comics were the primary literature sustaining my imagination (and attention) throughout my upbringing in Manila in the early 80s, when I became a ravenous collector after Papa took me to my first comics shop in Mannahatta during our family's inaugural visit to the U.S. We would join him in Westchester a few years later, when Mama put a ban on collecting because of her generational prejudice against comics' literary value. In 2005, I published my second book of poems, but felt psychically spent. Hollowed out by the ongoing U.S. war on terror, and put off by poetry factionalism and ethno/centrist gatekeeping, I found refuge and a renewed creative focus in comics. I would devote much of the proceeding years to absorbing its domestic and international histories, during which I would (re)discover the work of the artists mentioned earlier in this essay.

While visiting the Bay Area in support of my book, I was introduced by the visual artist Mel Vera Cruz to Abe Ignacio, Enrique de la Cruz, Jorge Emmanuel, and Helen Toribio's *The Forbidden Book: The Philippine-American War in Political Cartoons*, a soul-shaking history of American imperialism in the PI—a colony purchased from Spain for $20 million U.S. —lensed through the profoundly racist and jingoistic political cartoons appearing in various prominent American newspapers and magazines such as *LIFE* and *Harper's Weekly* between 1898 to 1903. Without question, *The Forbidden Book* inspires the meta-panel structure for *O.B.B.*, and emboldens the turns of my comics poem's (weird

I prepared my goodbyes

I began to let my mind wander

I was convinced this could be true

Two pages from a short-lived collaboration with Francis Estrada. Appears in New Yipes Reader No. 5, ed by Bruce Andrews, 2006.

postcolonial techno dreampop shoe)gaze at FilAm history, trans/nationalism, migration, desire, identity, melancholia, and shame.

¶ At the earliest stage of realizing *O.B.B.*, I knew that I didn't want to be the primary artist to generate its images. While I used to be an avid drawer, I gave up my practice around the time Mama kiboshed my comics habit. It also made no sense for me to work with a comics professional on a book whose terms of creation—improvisation, anti-narrativity, no deadlines— would fly in the face of industry norms. Aware that collaboration is at the heart of comics making history, I embraced this convention throughout the nearly two decades it's taken me to finish this book. Experimenting with five different artists, I would ultimately settle on the images generated with Ernest Concepcion and Alex Tarampi, whose art and illustrations span the reaches of analogue and digital.

Ernest and I met in 2005 at a party in the East Village, introduced by our friend Emmy Catedral, another Pilipinx artist and author. Like me, Ernest was born in Quezon City and grew up in Manila. He moved to the U.S. shortly after completing his studio art degree from UP, the same university my mother attended. When it comes to drawing, Ernest has few peers; his line is immediately recognizable, with talent to burn on the level of Keith Haring, Jean Giraud, Jason Pollan, and Katsuhiro Otomo. This would prove crucial to the early phase of *O.B.B.*, which called for an artist to keep up with my own improvisational and automatist process. During the summer of 2009, after years of working over email, Ernest and I finally made time to meet in his Gowanus studio. Over the course of three months, we generated an epic series of works on paper and acetate which, sadly, also marked the end of our collaboration. You'll see my hand in each piece of the series of poster-sized works in chapter 3, moments in *O.B.B.* when the roles of writer and artist intersect and overlap.

Alex Tarampi is a second generation Pilipinx American who grew up in Pennsylvania, completed a bachelor's degree in illustration and design at Pratt, and, until the fall of 2020, was living with his young family two blocks away from our apartment in Sunnyside, Queens. We began working together on *O.B.B.* before we became neighbors though, at the post-convention dinner hosted by our organizers of the first and only Asian American Comic Con at MoCCA back in 2009. (Come to think of it, we met at the same time that I was wrapping up my collaboration with Ernest in his

Gowanus studio. Talk about synchronicity.) I bonded with Alex over our love of Supes, Katsuhiro Otomo, and the world of HR Geiger. Unlike my work with Ernest, I would remain in the writer's lane for much of my collaboration with Alex, with the exception of the fifth chapter, where my collages serve as the foundation for his digital illustrations. I certainly enjoyed more in-person meetings with Alex because of our proximity to each other, enabling us to pore over together with greater frequency and ease whichever recent pages of text I'd send his way to illustrate. I love the circularity of *O.B.B.*, a comics poem that locates much of its play on ethno national identity in the space between the category of "Pilipinx" and "American" while its second half proceeds with the digital illustrations of a U.S.-born Pil Am illustrator raised in Philly. (Oh, you F's and P's!)

¶ Why poetry and comics? It would seem paradoxical to pair the two, given the gift economy of the former versus the latter's massive industry. Setting aside these disparities for the moment, let's consider bp Nichol's merging of both language arts as the progression of his interest to "write the way I draw and draw the way I write." Often in his comics, words exist two-dimensionally, like figures before a landscape. Simultaneously, in works such as "Scraptures 12," "Tegnikal Notes," "Bullsheets," "Lonely Fred," "MASQUE and Unmasking of Captain Poetry," Nichol will illustrate the contours of his figures with the delicate immediacy of calligraphy.

In his introduction to Nichol's essay "Comics as MYTH," Peters cites the poet's following assertion about "the relation between [an] overt use of space on the page and the structure of the poem," as something much more crucial than the fact of "a merely decorative use of letters," which "would scarcely justify a new style of poetry." Peters considers "this very 'relation'" the element "that is creative." It's reminiscent of Charles Hatfield's observation that readers' experience of comics as "radically fragmented and unstable" comprises "their great strength: comic art is composed of several kinds of tension, in which various ways of reading—various interpretive options and potentialities—must be played against each other."

Much of Nichol's comics are non-narrative, where the real "story" lies in the tension between the illustrated nature of the text and the written design of the image. Hatfield observes how "comics, like other hybrid texts, collapse the word/image dichotomy;" "visible language," he holds, can "be quite elaborate in appearance, forcing recognition of pictorial and material qualities that can be freighted with meaning…" But Nichol's comics embody the following idea recorded in his journal entry from 1964 AND with which he opens book 7 of *The Martyrology*:

> To go beyond THE WORD.
> exercise control over it? No
> NO NO—BEYOND THE
> WORD. not to merely control
> it but to overcome it, go be-
> yond the point where it is
> even necessary to think in
> terms of it (Nichol, *Gifts*, ii)

In book 1 of his magnum opus, Nichol writes:

> a future music moves now to be written
> w g r & t
> its form is not apparent
> it will be seen

With comics, Nichol's poem can "go be-/ yond the point where it is/ even necessary to think in/ terms of." His oeuvre can lay claim to a couple of formal breakthroughs: Canada's first original underground comics publication in "Scraptures 12," and comics poetry's first costumed superhero in *The Captain Poetry Poems Complete*.

¶ In April 2011, the influential Toronto small press Book*hug re-printed *The Captain Poetry Poems Complete* in a new edition that features an afterword by bill bissett, a poet and close friend of Nichol's whose blewointment press issued the original edition in 1971. A first in the genre of the superhero comics poem, *The Captain Poetry Poems Complete* reads with surprising immediacy and relevance. Outwardly, the book is highly reflective of the comics medium: not only does it predate and feature the same dimensions of current trades like *Arkham Asylum* and *Doom Patrol*, but also includes illustrations of our superhero on the front and back cover by an artist other than Nichol. Inside, the poems offer a hilarious deconstruction of the alpha-male superhero—nearly two decades before Alan Moore would attempt the same in *Miracleman* and *Watchmen*.

Shifting between the voice of the author, the omniscient narrator, ex-lovers, haters, and eyewitnesses, we are introduced to a Captain Poetry who is a romantic ("when did you learn/ Captain Poetry/ that you had placed her too high/ for even you/to fly"—(Captain Poetry, unpaginated); a "rye-bald" chauvinist pig—"now slaps her fanny/when he can;" a superhero who writes "trite" poetry that baldly mimics Robert Creeley—"O/ vellum stars/ he cries/(i./ e./ she's the one for/ he:" and an aspiring lothario who has to take out ads in the paper to score dates ("Attractive young man wearing/cape and hood wishes to meet/lady with similar interests./Object-mutual enjoyment"). According to Nichol, the idea behind the book

> was an attack on the macho male bullshit tradition in
> Canadian poetry where if you were male & wrote poems you
> had to make damn sure you could piss longer, shout harder,
> & drink more than any less obviously effete (i.e. they
> weren't writing poems) on this national block.

There's no mistaking Nichol's parody with the front cover illustration of CP, pounding his chest at the full moon, washboard abs defined, clad in nothing but a mask and speedo. CP's mask: a combless rooster head with a visor similar to X-Men's Cyclops. Hilariously, a wattle shaped like a pair of testicles dangles from his chin. But CP is a character whom Nichol won't disavow, because

> in certain ways i liked the idiot. & at certain points his
> idiocies became my own…but since i'm male & probably
> occasionally macho in spite of myself it's somewhat
> understandable that the parody slipped briefly into the
> subjective mode. one thing i do believe tho is that you let
> the mistakes stand.

¶ CP endears more in the second section of the book, "The Unmasking of Captain Poetry: a series of stills for dj." With the mask finally off, Nichol's superhero turns out to be none other than the poet's signature icon, Milt the Morph, who guest-appears in his other comics and cartoon strips. For much of this section, the page serves as the panel for the illustration or "still" that's printed on one side of the page, so that when we flip to the other side and find it blank, we can experience this moment like a pause or a beat prior to encountering the text-image on the following page.

This second section opens with an unmasked, smiling CP hiding inside the higher dimensions of the large case letter A, a variation of which we see four pages later. Inside these letter A's are mountains, clear skies, birds, trees—a natural world. Other stills include CP riding the letters, but with parts of the illustration whitened-out or erased, as if to suggest that anti-matter or negative space has entered the poem, but no problem—CP will continue to smile despite the crisis. The third and last page of the section feature panels, or "frames," as Nichol liked to call them. There is only a single frame on the third page, but seven on the last one, neither of which can contain CP; he not only stands outside, but in front of the two middle and bottom panels, with his feet planted on the fifth and laid out on the floor of the page like a doormat. The top row of panels and the left frame on the second row showcase scenes that include a celestial 2-dimensional letter B, a white picket fence with hints of mountains behind it, and a sunny sky filled with birds. Inexplicably, the remaining three frames are empty. Perhaps this might have to do with CP cleaning house? After all, his thought balloon reads: "like leaving my roots behind me!!!"

¶ Perhaps poetry and comics offer such an appealing hybrid language art to explore because of its potentially rich, as Nichol put it, "means by which to reach out and touch the other." Especially to a poet/artist like Nichol, a lay therapist by trade,

{t}he other is emerging as the necessary prerequisite for dialogues with the self that clarify the soul & heart and deepen the ability to love. {He} place{s him}self there, with them, whoever they are, wherever they are, who seek to reach themselves and the other thru the poem by as many exits and entrances as possible.

ACKNOWLEDGMENTS

---

bp Nichol, Ernie Chan, Jose Rizal, Frantz Fanon, Katsushika Hokusai, Raymond Queneau, Willam S. Burroughs, Richard Outcault, Nonoy Marcelo, Yoshihiro Togashi, Mariah Carey, Abe Ignacio, Enrique de la Cruz, Jorge Emmanuel, Helen Toribio, Lynda Barry, Shawn Carter, Osamu Tezuka, Yassan, Marcel Broodthaers, Craig Thompson, Manuel Auad, Max Ernst, Anne Anlin Cheng, Carl Craig, George Herriman, Sonja Ahlers, Richard Hahn, Keith Haring, Samuel R. Delany, Jean Giraud, Aline Crumb, Russell Tyrone Jones, Sandy Rivera, Pol Medina Jr, Jean Michel Basquiat, Alan Moore, Ralph Bakshi, Ariel Dorfman, Armand Mattelart, Thierry Groensteen, Margarita Alcantara-Tan, David Wojnarowicz, Hilary Chute, Heidi MacDonald, Grant Morrison, Joe Brainard, Melinda Gebbie, Algernon Blackwood, Sooyoung Park, Doug Martsch, Bernie Wrightson, Ray Johnson, Claude Cahun, Jess Collins, David Mazzuchelli, Dean Wareham, Damon Krukowski, Naomi Yang, Neil Gaiman, Theresa Hak Kyung Cha, Adrian Tomine, Lewis Klahr, Tamryn Bennett, Bern Porter, Ted Berrigan, Scott McCloud, Malcolm Macneil, Charles Hatfield, Art Spiegelman, Julie Doucet, Mariko Tamaki, Jillian Tamaki, Benedict Anderson, Vicente Rafael, Richard Baluyut, & Rosario Javier.

Maraming salamat kina Stephen, Lindsey, Rissa, Caelan, & Nightboat for championing *O.B.B.* and books like it.

A tentacular hug to Jill Magi and Sona for publishing "Goldfish Kisses" in their 2007 series of chapbooks.

Maraming salamat, Amy Sillman, for your brilliance, friendship, & generosity.

Maraming salamat, Millay Colony for the Arts, for the time, lodging, & space to work on the "Last Gasp" chapter of *O.B.B.*

Maraming salamat, Robert Rauschenberg Foundation, for your advocacy & support in this pandemic year.

Other poems + images from *O.B.B.* appear in the following journals & anthologies: *EDNA, LANA TURNER, MAKE Literary Magazine, POETRY, Poets of Queens* (QCA), *Queen's English,* & *Supplement: Volume 1.* Big shoutout to their editors: Cara Benson, David Lau, Cal Bedient, Chamandeep Bains, Fred Sasaki, Don Share, Olena Jennings, Kyoo Lee, James Sherry, & Orchid Tierney.

An early version of "Some Notes on bp Nichol, Poetry, & Comics" first appeared in *Reading the Difficulties: Dialogues with Contemporary American Innovative Poetry.* Salamat uli, Tom and Judith.

Realizing *O.B.B.* was made possible by the brilliant artistry, patience, & friendship of three O.B.B.s in my life. Ka Alex, Ernest, at Francis—ang utong na loob ko sa inyo e walang hanggaan.

O.B.B. pays homage to Tony de Zuñiga, Nestor Redondo, Alex Niño, Gerry Talaoc, Vic Catan, Alfredo Alcala, Francisco Coching, Ernie Chan, & the pioneering group of komikeros from the Philippines illustrating mainstream U.S. American comics in the 60s & 70s. Learn more about the trails they blazed for AAPI comics writers & artists in issue #4 of the *Comic Book Artist* (Vol. 2), published by TwoMorrows Press.

To my AAPI community & our allies—let's continue to center, love, & protect one another. We got this.

Finally, I dedicate this book to my family, &specially 明玉 —Baba's honey badger, Sith Lord, & *number one/in the setting sun.*

In loving memory of Mel Tobias (1939-2017) & Jim Wong-Chu (1949-2017)— dearest of mentors, protectors, & believers.

#StopAAPIHate #StopASIANHate #StandWITHAAPI #StandFORAsians

ABOUT THE AUTHOR

The former Queens Poet Laureate, Paolo Javier was born in the Philippines and grew up in Las Piñas, Manila; Katonah, Westchester County; El-Ma'adi, Cairo; Burnaby and North Delta, Vancouver. He has produced three albums of sound poetry with Listening Center, including the limited edition pamphlet/cassette *Ur'lyeh/Aklopolis* and the booklet/cassette *Maybe the Sweet Honey Pours*. Also a visual and sound artist, Javier received a Robert Rauschenberg Foundation Artist Fund Individual Grant in 2021 and has been a featured artist in MoMA PS1's 2015 Greater New York exhibition and Queen's Museum's 2018 Queens International exhibition. He is the author of four previous full-length books of poetry, including *the time at the end of this writing,* which received a Small Press Traffic Book of the Year Award, and *Court of the Dragon,* also published by Nightboat Books. He lives with his family in the unsurrendered territory of the Mespeatches, Munsee, Matinecock, Canarsie, and Rockaway Lenape, otherwise known as Queens, NYC.

ABOUT THE ARTISTS

Alexander Tarampi graduated from Pratt Institute and is an illustrator and web developer from Philadelphia. His work has appeared in *225 Plays: By The New York Neo-Futurists,* Paolo Javier's *Court of the Dragon, Secret Identities: The Asian American Superhero Anthology,* and his independently published comic book, *Millenisium.* http://theimaginary.net

Ernest Concepcion is a Filipino painter based in Manila, Philippines, who combines the motif of classical landscape with contemporary caricatures and representations that take one into the framework of warfare while uncovering the effects of a larger 20th-Century, Postwar existence. https://ernestconcepcion.com

Francis Estrada was born in the Philippines and moved to America in 1988. He currently lives in Brooklyn, NY. He is a visual artist, museum educator, freelance art educator, and traditional Filipinx martial arts instructor. https://www.francisestrada.com

NIGHTBOAT BOOKS

Nightboat Books, a nonprofit organization, seeks to develop audiences for writers whose work resists convention and transcends boundaries. We publish books rich with poignancy, intelligence, and risk. Please visit nightboat.org to learn about our titles and how you can support our future publications.

The following individuals have supported the publication of this book. We thank them for their generosity and commitment to the mission of Nightboat Books:

Kazim Ali
Anonymous (4)
Abraham Avnisan
Jean C. Ballantyne
The Robert C. Brooks Revocable Trust
Amanda Greenberger
Rachel Lithgow
Anne Marie Macari
Elizabeth Madans
Elizabeth Motika
Thomas Shardlow
Benjamin Taylor
Jerrie Whitfield & Richard Motika

This book is made possible, in part, by grants from the New York City Department of Cultural Affairs in partnership with the City Council and the New York State Council on the Arts Literature Program.

12/21